T0328680

Cambridge Elements ≡

Elements in Religion and Monotheism
edited by
Paul K. Moser
Loyola University Chicago
Chad Meister
*Affiliate Scholar, Ansari Institute for Global Engagement with Religion,
University of Notre Dame*

JEWISH MONOTHEISM AND SLAVERY

Catherine Hezser
SOAS University of London

CAMBRIDGE
UNIVERSITY PRESS

CAMBRIDGE
UNIVERSITY PRESS

Shaftesbury Road, Cambridge CB2 8EA, United Kingdom

One Liberty Plaza, 20th Floor, New York, NY 10006, USA

477 Williamstown Road, Port Melbourne, VIC 3207, Australia

314–321, 3rd Floor, Plot 3, Splendor Forum, Jasola District Centre,
New Delhi – 110025, India

103 Penang Road, #05–06/07, Visioncrest Commercial, Singapore 238467

Cambridge University Press is part of Cambridge University Press & Assessment,
a department of the University of Cambridge.

We share the University's mission to contribute to society through the pursuit of
education, learning and research at the highest international levels of excellence.

www.cambridge.org
Information on this title: www.cambridge.org/9781009500333

DOI: 10.1017/9781009260497

First published 2024

A catalogue record for this publication is available from the British Library.

ISBN 978-1-009-50033-3 Hardback
ISBN 978-1-009-26050-3 Paperback
ISSN 2631-3014 (online)
ISSN 2631-3006 (print)

Jewish Monotheism and Slavery

Elements in Religion and Monotheism

DOI: 10.1017/9781009260497
First published online: February 2024

Catherine Hezser
SOAS University of London
Author for correspondence: Catherine Hezser, ch12@soas.ac.uk

Abstract: Biblical monotheism imagines God as a slave master who owns and has total control over humans as his slaves, who are expected to show obedience to him. The theological use of slavery metaphors has a limited value, however, and is deeply problematic from the perspective of real-life slave practices. Ancient authors already supplemented the metaphor of God as a slave master with other images and emphasized God's difference from human slave owners. Ancient and modern experiences of and attitudes toward slavery determined the understanding and applicability of the slavery metaphors. This Element examines the use of slavery metaphors in ancient Judaism and Christianity in the context of the social reality of slavery, modern abolitionism, and historical-critical approaches to the ancient texts.

Keywords: slavery, monotheism, Jewish, Christian, Bible

ISBNs: 9781009500333 (HB), 9781009260503 (PB), 9781009260497 (OC)
ISSNs: 2631-3014 (online), 2631-3006 (print)

Contents

Introduction

God as a Slave Master

The tradents and editors of the Hebrew Bible presented the Israelite God in terms that were known to them from their own life experiences and social relationships. One such experience was slavery. Especially in the prophetic and poetic books of the Hebrew Bible and also already in the book of Genesis God is imagined and addressed as a male householder and slave master (*adonai* = "my master"), with the patriarchs, kings, and ordinary Israelites as his slaves (sg. *eved*, pl. *avadim*). For example, when God reveals himself as Abraham's protector (or "shield," Gen. 15:1) in a vision, Abraham addresses him as his "master" (*Adonai Yahveh*, Gen. 15:2). In Psalms, not only Abraham (e.g., Ps. 105:6) but also David (e.g., Ps. 18:1, 36:1) is presented as the slave of God (*eved Yahveh*) and the slave metaphor is used dozens of times as a form of self-identification of human beings before God (e.g., Ps. 19:14, 27:9, 31:17, 34:23, 69:18).

The field of images (*Bildfeld*) associated with slavery functioned in and received its meanings and associations from an ancient socioeconomic context in which slavery and slave practices were an everyday phenomenon. By imagining and addressing God as their master, the ancient Israelite authors of these texts expressed the great hierarchical difference between humans and God and evoked certain attributes associated with human masters that they conferred onto God. According to Lockyer (1975: 15–16), these attributes included the notions of authority, power, reverence, and responsibility. God's total control over human beings is also part of the image: His treatment of humans included both praise and correction, even if the latter led to the person's death. Yet the more negative practices of human slave owners, such as the suppression and abuse of their subordinates, are omitted in the use of the metaphor for God.

From the perspective of humans, the image of the slave evokes the connotations of subservience, submission, and lowliness (Bridge 2010: 50–51). Another important aspect is obedience: Like a slave serving his master, Israelites were expected to obey God and fulfil the commandments and laws he had issued (Ex. 19–23: the revelation of Torah law at Sinai). If they failed, they had to reckon with severe punishment. The most debilitating aspects of enslavement are absent from the image of humans as God's "slaves." Even as "slaves" of God, humans possess agency and free will. The biblical image of God as a slave master and humans as his slaves therefore has its limits, which are also evident in the complementary use of other metaphors from the field of social relationships, namely that of the father vis-à-vis his children and that of the judge and those who appear before him in court.

The view of God as a slave master was not limited to ancient Israelite religion and monotheism. The name or title Adonai has analogies in polytheistic religions of the Ancient Near East. Lockyer refers to the Phoenician god Adonis and to Baal as the title of Canaanite gods (Lockyer 1975: 15), both of whom were known to the Israelites and appear as parts of divine (Adoni-jah) and human names (Ish-baal, Baal-jah). Adonis was imagined as a beautiful youth, however, and became most prominent as Aphrodite's lover in later Greek myth (Ferguson 2003: 277). Associations of domination and slavery are more pronounced in the local Syrian cult of Baal ("owner," "overlord"), a fertility god whose worship involved sexual slavery and prostitution (Amos 2:7–9; Devries 1997: 80). Baal appeared in various local configurations and embodiments in Semitic religious contexts (Sommer 2009: 24–26). At times, Israelites are associated with his worship (see, for example, Num. 25:3, Judges 10:6). Hybrid religious practices that merged the Jewish God with Baal (and other Canaanite gods) evoked prophetic criticism (e.g., Hosea 4:12; Perdue 2013: 184) but seem to have continued in Hellenistic times. According to the Hebrew version of 1 Maccabees 1:54, in 167 BCE, an image of Baal Shamayim ("Master of Heavens") was set up in the Jerusalem Temple by Antiochus IV Epiphanes – with the support of the high priest Menelaos and Jewish Hellenizers – and considered an "abomination" by the Maccabees (see also Daniel 9:23–27).

The Limits of Theology

Obviously, all human talk about God is conducted in human language and based on human experiences. It is therefore always problematic, potentially misleading, and incomplete. This phenomenon has led to a fundamental criticism of any kind of "theology," especially that which involves anthropomorphism, among some modern Jewish philosophers such as Abraham Joshua Heschel and Yeshayahu Leibowitz. Heschel (1951: 61) points to "the tension of the known and the unknown, of the common and the holy, of the nimble and the ineffable," Therefore, "all perception is an externalization, ... the essence begins where perception ends" (Heschel 1951: 63). While emphasizing God's transcendence and otherness, Heschel also points to the this-worldly traces of the Divine that inspire awe. Perhaps even more stringently, based on Maimonides' emphasis on "the absolute transcendence of God," Yeshayahu Leibowitz points to the limitations of human knowledge of the Divine and represents an "agnostic type of theology," in which God can be known through the perception of "his works, that is, the natural order of things" alone (Goldman 1992: xiv). Negative theology, that is, the radical distinction of the Divine from everything that is human and the rejection of anthropomorphic attributes, has become the hall-mark of modern Jewish thought, especially after the Holocaust: "theologians of the *via negativa* argue that descriptive characteristics such as living, loving, good, or wise are not essentially constitutive of God's nature; or else they deny that the essential divine nature can be known to us as such" (Fagenblat 2017: 2). From this perspective, the biblical perception of God as a slave master would be considered inadequate.

Ancient rabbis, for whom the Hebrew Bible was divinely inspired and its representation of God constitutive, bridged this seeming contradiction between the known and unknown God by telling parables that likened God to a "king of flesh and blood," who could be imagined as a householder and slave owner. In the parable's application (*nimshal*), the likeness between God and this most powerful human being could be expressed in an affirmative or negative way, depending on the latter's behavior and the circumstances involved (Thoma 1989: 39; Teugels 2019: 277–280, 292–296). While some of the parables compare God to a human slave master, who gives orders but also praises and rewards his slaves, the *via negativa* parables emphasize that God behaves differently (Hezser 2005: 346–362 and 2023). Thus, the image of the human slave owner could be used to express the Jewish God's otherness.

Another strategy was the combination of distinct and partly contradictory metaphors, such as that of the strict slave owner and loving father, which are used side by side in the Hebrew Bible already. A midrashic parable (Pesiqta Rabbati 27[28]) states that God will treat those who do his will as a father treats his child, "but if not, he will force you and you are his slave." The midrash quotes Jeremiah 2:14, where the question is posed: "Is Israel a slave? Is he a home-born slave?" In both the biblical (Jer. 2:13) and the rabbinic contexts, the slavery metaphor is linked to wrongdoing. Those who transgress God's commandments may experience him as a harsh slave master who does not spare his slaves severe punishment. In this literary context the metaphor of God as a slave master is used to admonish humans to follow God's commandments. The slavery metaphor reveals the negative, threatening side of God, whom one may otherwise experience as a kind, supportive, and forgiving father.

The master–slave imagery also reveals another aspect of ancient Israelite and Jewish religion, namely, the collaborative and complementary nature of the relationship between God and humans. As Heschel (1959: 51) has pointed out, the covenantal relationship means that "God is in need of man" to create a world and society that is worth living in. Just as a slave master is dependent on the work that his slaves carry out for him, God needs humans to labor for the betterment of the world so that *tikkun olam* ("repair of the world") can be achieved. This notion of collaboration is emphasized in the kabbalistic tradition, in which human behavior in this world, whether good or bad, has an impact on the movement of divine powers (Dan 1986: 14 and 23). As Ariel has pointed out, according to kabbalistic thought, "God ... depends on us"; "human actions ... cause God to respond involuntarily ... These responses then produce reverberations that rebound from God to man" (Ariel 2006: 18). Thus, "[t]he novel element in *Kabbalistic* thinking about God and man is their mutual and reciprocal interdependence" (Ariel 2006: 18). Slavery metaphors continue to be used in the *Zohar*, the most important work of Jewish mysticism, created in the thirteenth century (Giller 2001: 44). An innovation is the emphasis on spiritual enslavement, which is considered to lead to bodily enslavement in the form of persecution by other nations. In turn, the experience of such "enslavement" is thought to accelerate spiritual perfection (Laitman 2007: 343–344). In earlier *Hekhalot* texts, the mysterious figure of Metatron is presented as God's "boy" (*na'ar*), "slave" (*eved*), and "beloved servant" (*shamashah rehima*), who is an angelic being superior to human beings ("Prince of the World") but inferior to God (Orlov 2005: 135 and Orlov 2005: 135 no. 228).

The use of slavery metaphors in Jewish literature from the Bible to the Zohar is based on the practice and experience of slavery in the ancient and medieval world (Bradley & Cartledge 2011; Perry et al. 2021). For the ancient and medieval readers and listeners, real-life connotations and experiences of enslavement would have determined their understanding of the texts. Besides the metaphorical use of "slave" and "master" for humans' relationship to God, ancient Jewish texts also frequently mention mundane slave–master relationships and slavery practices the tradents and editors were familiar with (Hezser 2005). In these texts, ancient Israelites and Jews of the Hellenistic, Roman, and Sasanian periods appear as both slaveholders and slaves. They were enslaved, in the literal sense of the word, by both non-Jewish and Jewish masters and owned both Jewish ("Hebrew") and non-Jewish ("Canaanite") slaves. Slavery was pervasive in the ancient Middle East and in Persian, Greek, and Roman societies. The question is whether and to what extent Israelites and Jews perceived slavery differently from other social groups, based on biblical monotheism with its distinct legal rules, ethics, and theology (Hezser 2022). If God was perceived as one's only master, how could one be enslaved to a worldly master? If enslavement was considered disastrous, how could one inflict it on others? Did Jews treat (some of) their slaves more mildly than non-Jewish owners and if so, what was their behavior based on?

The Biblical Exodus Tradition: Liberation from Enslavement

Crucial for an understanding of the significance of slavery in Jewish monotheism is the Exodus experience related in the biblical book of Exodus. The Israelites had settled in Egypt since Joseph was sold into servitude by his brothers (Gen. 37:27) and brought to Pharaoh's court, where he was promoted to the high administrative office of governor (Gen. 41:43–44, 42:6). Later a famine brought his father Jacob-Israel and his brothers to Egypt (Gen. 42–50). Whereas relations between Israelites and Egyptians are described as friendly and welcoming in Genesis (Gen. 50:50: when Jacob died, "the Egyptians wept for him"), in Exodus the situation has changed. The Egyptians now consider the Israelites foreign intruders and oppress them: "And the Egyptians enslaved the children of Israel ruthlessly. And they made their lives bitter with hard work, in mortar and in brick, and in all kinds of work in the field; [in] all their works in which they worked [they made them work] ruthlessly" (Ex. 1:13–14). Eventually Moses, to whom God introduces himself in a vision (Ex. 3:3–6), functions as the leader who guides the Israelites out of their servitude and persecution in Egypt, in accordance with God's plan for them: "And I have come down to rescue them from the hand of the Egyptians and to bring them up from that land to a good and wide land, a land flowing with milk and honey" (Ex. 3:8). Moses' role is that of an intermediary and executor of God's will.

In the book of Exodus, Israelite monotheism (or monolatry, that is, the Israelite's worship of Yahweh as their God) are closely linked: Yahweh introduces himself as the God who delivers them from slavery in Egypt. The covenantal relationship (Ex. 6:4–5, 19:5) and revelation of the Torah at Sinai (Ex. 19–24) are interwoven into the Exodus from Egypt toward the promised land. God's covenant is with the Israelites as a free people and as such they are obliged to fulfil God's commandments. One of these commandments concerns the essence of Israelite monotheism/monolatry: "I am Yahweh, your God, who brought you out of the land of Egypt, from the house of slaves [*bet avadim*]. You shall not have any other gods besides me" (Ex. 20:2–3). The Israelite God introduces himself as the only master of a people liberated from slavery here. As long as they were slaves of the Egyptians and had to obey the commands of human masters, proper worship of the Israelite God would have been impossible. The liberation from slavery sets the stage for the Israelites' exclusive service to God as their divine master and commitment to his commandments.

The Exodus in Collective Memory

From antiquity onward this foundational experience within ancient Israelite religious history became part of Israelite and Jewish collective memory. Already in Ex. 13:3 Moses instructs the Israelites: "Remember this day, on which you came out of Egypt, from the house of slaves [*bet avadim*]. For by strength of hand Yahweh brought you out of there." The "hand" of God succeeded over the "hand of the Egyptians" (cf. Ex. 3:8). Not only in the Torah but also in the prophetic books Egypt stands for slavery and oppression and the Exodus experience for divine deliverance (e.g., Isa. 11:16 and 19; Jer. 2:6, 7:25, 11:4.7, 16:14; Ez. 20:5–10). As the most important salvific experience of the past, the remembrance of the Exodus can raise hopes for a better future, free from various types of worldly oppression, and is also associated with messianic times (Chen 2019: 146).

The Passover holiday is already mentioned in the Torah as an annual day of commemoration of the Exodus experience: "And this day shall be for a memorial (*zikaron*) for you, and you shall observe it as a holiday to Yahweh throughout your generations; you shall keep it a holiday by an ordinance forever" (Ex. 12:14). Rather than merely commemorating a past experience, self-identification with the Exodus generation involved a constant actualization of the notion of liberation from slavery. The Mishnah, the first compilation of rabbinic traditions edited around 200 CE, rules: "In every generation a person is obliged to see himself as if he came out of Egypt, as it is said: 'And you shall tell your son on that day: It is because of that which the Lord did for me when I came out of Egypt' [Ex. 13:8]. .... He brought us forth from slavery to freedom, ..., from servitude to redemption" (m. Pes. 10:4). As Bokser (1984: 72–73) has already pointed out, the aspect of redemption is expanded in the Mishnah and related to the situation of Jews after the destruction of the Second Temple in 70 CE. In the discussion of the blessing to be recited during the Passover *seder* (m. Pes. 10:6), "Aqiva ... refers to an ever-recurring redemption that applies not only to the ancient Israelites but also to the current generation" (Bokser 1984: 73). At the time when Palestinian Jewish subjugation to Rome was perceived as political slavery and capture by Roman soldiers could lead to real enslavement (Hezser 2005: 220–233), the Passover message had a socioeconomic and political meaning. It expressed the hope for future physical, spiritual, and political freedom and independence from foreign dominion.

The continued significance of the Exodus story in late antique and early Byzantine times is also evident from the artistic use of Exodus-related motifs on the wall of the Dura Europos synagogue and the mosaic floors of the recently discovered Huqoq and Wadi Hamam synagogues. Whereas a Dura Europos wall painting depicts Moses in the midst of the departing Israelites and drowning Egyptians, the Huqoq and Wadi Hamam mosaics show only God's punishment of the Egyptians: Pharaoh's soldiers and chariots are drowning and struggling with fish in the Red Sea. The artistic renderings would have reminded Jewish viewers of God's salvific power in the context of the oppressive Byzantine Christian rule (Hezser, forthcoming).

Slavery in the Bible and Modern Abolitionism

How can the religious emphasis on liberation from slavery and the notion of God as one's only master be reconciled with the actual experience and practice of slavery in ancient Jews' daily lives? Earlier scholars of ancient Judaism often tried to dismiss the existence of slavery practices in ancient Israelite and Jewish culture, especially as far as Jewish slaves held by Jewish owners were concerned. Studies of slaves and slavery in the Hebrew Bible and postbiblical Jewish literature began in the middle of the nineteenth century, when the abolition of slavery was discussed and eventually enacted by law in America (13th Amendment to the US Constitution in 1865; Slavery Abolition Act in Britain in 1833). One of the earliest scholars who wrote about slavery in ancient Judaism was Moses Mielziner (1828–1903), an American Reform rabbi who was born in Prussia, Germany, and came to America in 1865. He became a professor of Talmud and rabbinic literature at Hebrew Union College, the Reform rabbinical school, in Cincinnati in 1879 and succeeded Isaac Meyer Wise in the presidency of the institution in 1900.

While some American Jews were slave owners (Faber 1998; Friedman 1998; Drescher 2010), American Jews were much involved in the abolitionist movement, foremost among them Reform Jews. As Garlitz (2015: 574) has pointed out: "The Jewish abolitionists were primarily Reform Jews because the issues surrounding abolition appeared related to the problems Reform Judaism faced in the mid-nineteenth century. ... Many of Europe's Reform Jews became abolitionists in America after immigration." Experiences of anti-Semitism and discrimination in Europe made them sympathize with Blacks as victims of racism: "The Jewish abolitionists made telling parallels between Poland, Russia, the Germanic states, and America; between women and Blacks, and Jews and Blacks" (Sokolov 2010: 139). Another contributing factor was Reform Judaism's emphasis on ethical monotheism, in competition with Christian Protestantism's association of moral values with Jesus. According to the Reform thinker Moritz Lazarus' *The Ethics of Judaism* (1889), "God represents the 'source and archetype of the moral idea' or even 'the moral idea itself'"(Meyer 1997: 204). That the biblical God could have tolerated and condoned slavery was difficult to reconcile with the ethical monotheism ideal.

Therefore, the Hebrew Bible was interpreted in an apologetic way that supported the antislavery stance: "Jewish abolitionists denied a pro-slavery interpretation of the Bible and rejected racialist thinking that emphasized a contrast of stereotypes. Abolitionists practicing Reform Judaism tended to believe that their religion had a special mission in the world and that it predicated the notion of social justice in some capacity" (Garlitz 2015: 574).

In his study of the Bible's position on slavery, submitted in German and Latin to the University of Giessen as a doctoral thesis, Moses Mielziner (1859: 7, 1931: 64) wrote: "Among the religions and legislations of antiquity none could exhibit a spirit so decidedly averse to slavery as the religion and legislation of Moses; nor could any ancient nation find, in the circumstances of its own origin, such powerful motives to abolish that institution as the people of Israel." Once an English translation was made without Mielziner's knowledge and published in the *American Theological Review* of April 1861, the work "was avidly seized upon by leaders of the abolitionist movement in the United States, who, like Francis Lieber, felt that Mielziner's dissertation 'effectively knocked the divinity of the institution [of slavery] into a cocked hat'" (B.E.J. 1932: 152).

Mielziner argued that the biblical ideas of human dignity, "most tender kindness … especially toward the needy and the unfortunate," and ancient Israelites' own experience of slavery in Egypt indicated an abolitionist ideal in the Hebrew Bible already (Mielziner 1859: 7, 1931: 64). Since slavery was all pervasive at that time, they were unable to fully accomplish their goals. In the context of ancient slave practices, they differed from other nations by treating their slaves more mildly and releasing Hebrew slaves in the seventh year. Mielziner's study was cited by Christian Old Testament scholars, who saw their own views supported by his arguments.

Thus, Oehler (1891: 382) argues that the creation of humans in God's likeness and universal descendance from Adam as the first human make slavery as practiced by other ancient people impossible among Israelites. While the patriarchs are said to have owned slaves, the relationship between slaves and their masters was "ennobled" (orig. German: "veredelt") by their kind treatment of slaves (Oehler 1891: 383). Oddly enough, Oehler refers to the commandment to circumcise non-Jewish male slaves (Gen. 17: 12–13) as an example of their allegedly favorable treatment, believing that their circumcision meant their full integration into the divine covenant with the Israelites (Oehler 1891: 383), when it was merely a precondition for serving in Israelite households (Hezser 2005: 35–41). Oehler justifies the biblical distinction between Hebrew and Canaanite slaves by pointing to the Israelites as God's "native people" ("Eigentumsvolk"), who, as a consequence of their liberation from slavery in Egypt (Exodus), are forever free from all human enslavement (Oehler 1891: 383). The biblical contradiction between the Exodus experience and slave practices that involve both Israelite and non-Israelite slaves is "resolved" by negating the reality of Israelites owning Hebrew slaves ("With this principle [the Exodus as liberation from slavery] bondage ["Leibeigenschaft"] is, strictly speaking, abrogated for Israel," [Oehler 1891: 383], my translation from the German). Since he considers non-Israelite slaves partaking in some of Israel's blessings *qua* circumcision, the Hebrew Bible advocates their humane treatment (Oehler 1891: 384).

This approach, which may be considered wishful thinking or the whitewashing of slave practices mentioned in the foundational "Holy Scriptures" of Judaism and Christianity, mostly continued until the 1960s and 1970s (see, for example, König 1873/4; Grünfeld 1886; Farbstein 1896; Krauss 1911/1966: 83). For Jewish and Christian scholars who considered slavery morally wrong, it was inconceivable that biblical scriptures could take slavery for granted as a part of everyday life experience whose legitimacy was not questioned by the tradents and editors of the texts. To understand their arguments properly, it is necessary to also look at anti-abolitionists' use of biblical slavery texts (Giles 1994; Haynes 2002), however. For example, the Christian reverent Priest (1852: 561) maintained that Scripture "permits" and "tolerates" the institution of slavery, even if it does not "sanction" it: "no where does it command masters to manumit their slaves." Ancient Jews and Christians held slaves and were nevertheless members of God's covenant and church (Priest 1852: 561). Therefore, the arguments of abolitionists are deemed inappropriate: "Now, let our anti-slavery brethren produce us a declaration . . . that slavery, which Moses tolerated, is no longer *tolerated*, that no slaveholder shall be a deacon, a presbyter, or a bishop" (Priest 1852: 563). Contributing to American (anti-) abolitionist discussions, Smith (1863: 6) went even further by maintaining "that the Old Testament distinctly recognizes Slavery as a Hebrew institution" and "that Slavery is a divine institution established by God for all time." Anti-abolitionist preachers admonished slaves to obey their masters, claiming that slavery was a God-willed institution (Vile 2020: 161). Noll (2006: 2) has pointed to the American Civil War as a "theological crisis" over the proper interpretation of the Bible. Both abolitionists and their opponents used references to slaves and slavery in the Hebrew Bible in support of their irreconcilable positions on the most important humanitarian and socioeconomic issue of their time. While we may dismiss their approaches as ideological rather than scholarly, the historical and theological problem of the (ir)reconcilability of Jewish and Christian monotheism with slavery remains.

Modern Historical-Critical Approaches

In the 1960s and 1970s, approaches to slavery in the Bible became more critical, not least because of the development of historical-critical methodologies that analyze ancient texts in the political, socioeconomic, and cultural contexts (*Sitz im Leben*) in which they were formulated and within the literary contexts in which they appear (*Sitz in der Literatur*). Scholars who apply these methodologies are able to view ancient Jewish texts about slaves and slavery within the context of ancient slave practices and in the redactional contexts of the respective documents rather than from contemporary ideological perspectives. Like the representation of women in the Bible and other ancient texts, the representation of slaves is evaluated in the context of ancient patriarchal and slave-holding societies whose values, conditions, and experiences differed significantly from our own.

Other developments of the 1960s and 1970s were also crucial for a change in perspective. This was the time of the student revolts against social injustice and inequality and of the American civil rights movement fighting for equal rights for Black Americans. Black civil rights leaders such as Martin Luther King (1929–68) identified with biblical slaves and likened the Exodus of ancient Israelites from Egypt to Black Americans' struggle for equality (Miller 2012: 84–85). Scholars and public figures became more sensitive and outspoken about the treatment and representation of groups subjected to white male dominance, such as slaves, women, and people of color, with some people suffering from inequalities on several counts. It also became evident that freedom from slavery did not necessarily lead to social integration and legal equality, since racism continued. In the decades after the Holocaust, Jewish suffering and oppression by the German National Socialists and the widespread use of forced labor to dominate subjected populations had become public knowledge. Greater public awareness for the subjugation, abuse, and exploitation of minorities and all those who did not belong to the powerful and dominant white male elites sensitized academics to inequalities in other historical periods. Hence, the representation of slaves in the Bible and other foundational texts was reexamined.

In his study of "Slavery in the Old Testament," van der Ploeg (1972: 75) analyzed the use of servile terminology in the Hebrew Bible and concluded that "[t]he most common meaning of 'eved is 'slave.' The slaves were the possession of their masters, who had captured, bought, inherited them." Slavery was practiced by the ancient Israelites because it "belonged to the social pattern of the Near East" (Ploeg 1972: 76–77). At the same time, slave practices varied from one society to the next and in various locations and time periods. Therefore, the respective historical, political, socioeconomic, and cultural context is decisive for a proper understanding of references to slaves and slavery in ancient Jewish texts. Whereas the Hebrew Bible "did not attempt to overthrow the *ius gentium* concerning slavery," it "attempt[ed] to raise the position of the Israelite slave" and "also tried to raise the situation of the alien slave as a human being" (Ploeg 1972: 87).

Among Jewish Studies scholars Zeitlin and Urbach were the first who examined ancient Jewish slavery from a critical perspective, with a focus on postbiblical Jewish Hellenistic and rabbinic texts. Zeitlin (1962–3) emphasized that there were both shared and distinct features as far as slave practices and attitudes toward slavery in Jewish other ancient societies are concerned: "The Stoic philosophers and the Jewish sages taught that slaves are human beings and should be accorded humane treatment but they did not advocate their abolition" (Zeitlin 1962–3: 185). Both the Bible and the rabbinic texts "sanctioned the institution of slavery" but introduced regulations that limited its impact (e.g., Jewish slaves to be released in the seventh or Sabbatical Year) and mitigated against a harsh and exploitative treatment of slaves (e.g., with regard to the punishment of slaves). Zeitlin distinguished between Jewish sources from different time periods (Hebrew Bible, Philo, Josephus, tannaitic texts) and detected contradictions (e.g., concerning the enslavement of a debtor who could not repay his creditor) and developments (especially in the humane treatment of slaves) over time. Like Zeitlin, Urbach (1964: 4) notes that "slavery was taken for granted as a factor basic to political, social, and economic life" and Jews "formed no exception." Under certain circumstances such as poverty and debts, Jews could become the slaves of Jewish masters. Urbach's assumption that this phenomenon was limited to pre-Maccabean times is not persuasive, however, since later rabbinic texts know of such relationships as well (Hezser 2005: 6).

Slavery in Rabbinic and Early Christian Texts

In the last decades, the contextual approach, which views ancient Jewish literary sources on slavery within their respective ancient political, socioeconomic, legal, and cultural environments, has benefitted from studies on slaves and slavery in ancient Near Eastern (Mendelsohn 1978; Chirichigno 1993), Greek (Lewis 2018; Forsdyke 2021; Owens 2022; Kamen 2023), and Roman societies (Bradley 1994; Joshel 2010; Harper 2011). My own study of Jewish slavery in antiquity (Hezser 2005) focuses on rabbinic texts and examines them in the context of Graeco-Roman legal rules, attitudes, and practices. Based on the literary sources, Jewish slave law, practices, and attitudes toward slaves differed from those of surrounding societies in several regards (Hezser 2022): (1) Debt slavery and self-sale continued to be practiced in Jewish Palestine in the first centuries CE. They would have been caused by extreme poverty and the loss of landed property because of the Roman occupation, droughts, and inheritance issues. (2) Non-Jewish male slaves were circumcised and female slaves immersed by their Jewish owners, but these rituals did not constitute conversion of the slave to Judaism. Rather, they enabled them to work in Jewish households, where purity and kashrut rules were observed. (3) The children of free male Jews and slave women had the status of slaves. This rule served to maintain the boundaries of the nuclear Jewish family and limited the number of legitimate heirs. (4) Rabbis advocated mildness toward slaves, both as far as their everyday life treatment and punishments were concerned. They did not share Roman legal notions of the owner's power over his slave's life and death and advised masters to properly nourish their slaves and enable them to rest.

Most importantly, rabbis stress the humanity of slaves and their creation in the image of God, like free human beings (y. Ketub. 5:5, 30a: quotation of Job 31:15: "Did not He who made me in the womb make him?"). The biblical distinctions between Hebrew/Jewish and Canaanite/non-Jewish slaves are generally absent from rabbinic slave law and appear in exegetical contexts only (McCraken Flesher 1988; Hezser 2005: 27–35). Wealthy Jewish householders would have owned both Jewish and non-Jewish slaves (Rosenfeld & Perlmutter 2020: 76, 139, and 163 for the period of the Mishnah). As in Roman law, in rabbinic halakhah the distinction between free(born) persons and slaves is crucial, whereas ethnic distinctions among slaves became increasingly irrelevant. As free male Jewish householders, rabbis distinguished themselves from slaves, who were not even included in the rabbinic construction of a social hierarchy of Jewish society. All rabbinic texts are formulated from the perspective of rabbis as free male intellectuals, even if not all of them belonged to the economic elite as Roman writers, jurists, and philosophers did.

Glancy (2002) has shown that slavery was ubiquitous in early Christianity. The use of slaves in parables and the notion of spiritual slavery are understandable on the background of slave practices in Christian society only. Paul's allegation that spiritual slavery (of those who are not believers in Christ) is what really matters (see, for example, Gal. 4:7) not only disregards the seriousness of physical slavery but also sanctions it (Glancy 2002: 38). This is also the case with his claim that among those who are Christian "there is neither Jew nor Greek, there is neither slave nor free, there is no male and female, for all of you are one in Jesus Christ" (Gal. 3:27–28). Such illusional oneness "in spirit" accepts social hierarchies and power differences as natural and sanctioned by God rather than suggesting that real slavery should be abolished and that women and men should be treated equally within society. Paul shared the notion of human kinship and the danger of enslavement to evil forces within oneself (e.g., desires and emotions) with Stoic philosophers: "the Stoics held that a common rationality resulted in the kinship of all people, master and slave" (Risinger 2021: 157). Therefore, slaves could become "masters" of their emotions, whereas free people could remain "enslaved" to them. Both Paul and the

Stoics use these metaphors to admonish others to become like them, that is, to become believers in Christ (Paul) or followers of Stoicism. Real-life slave practices were left unchanged by these ideas.

According to Kyrtatas (1987: 41), "early Christian attitudes to slavery . . . did not provide an incentive to slaves to join the churches." He rejects the often-repeated notion that "slaves were numerous in the early Christian communities" (Kyrtatas 1987: 41). In fact, "rural slaves are nowhere reported to have been converted to Christianity throughout our period." Similarly, household slaves would hardly have been in a leisurely position in which they could devote themselves to spiritual causes. Therefore, "the general impression [is] that the early Christian communities did not include slaves" (Kyrtatas 1987: 43). Glancy points to another issue, namely, "the (in)compatibility between enslaved and thus sexually vulnerable bodies and the strictures of purity demanded within the Christian body" (Glancy 2002: 40). In reality, then, being a slave was incompatible with being a religious Jew or Christian in antiquity. Not only were slaves associated with *porneia* by being sexually available (Glancy 2002: 50–59), they also had to obey human masters more than they were able to obey God. The image of slaves as "blank slates" who were "inscribed" by their masters enabled them to become integral parts of Christian (Meeks 1983, 2nd ed. 2003: 63–64) and Jewish households (Hezser 2005: 123–148; Sivertsev 2005: 238). It did not make them "proper" Jews or Christians, however, and it is unlikely that they were treated as religious equals by their masters. It therefore seems that both social and religious distinctions between slaves and freeborn people generally continued in ancient Jewish and Christian societies.

Ramelli (2016) has shown that certain ancient Jewish and Christian ascetic groups such as the Essenes (Murphy 2002: 416) and Therapeutai (first c. BCE to first c. CE), mentioned by Philo and Josephus, Syrian Christian ascetics, and Gregory of Nyssa (fourth c. CE), differed from their "mainstream" coreligionists in their outspoken opposition to slavery. Members of such "sectarian" minority groups questioned the legitimacy of slavery as part of their rejection of wealth and material possessions and on the basis of their eschatological beliefs. In contrast to other bishops and church fathers, who endorsed slavery and considered it "useful to life" (Theodoret), Gregory of Nyssa considered the creation of all humans in the image of God and the notion of the Exodus as redemption from slavery incompatible with slave practices. He did not own slaves himself. Nevertheless, "nobody in antiquity and late antiquity seems to have campaigned to change the law and make slavery illegal" (Ramelli 2016: 2).

Slavery and Gender

One aspect of the contextual approach to ancient slavery is the greater attention to gender differences among slaves. Murnaghan and Joshel (1998) were groundbreaking in their study of striking similarities and differences between slaves, women, and children as dependents of the free male householder in Graeco-Roman society. Similar "differential equations" can be found in rabbinic texts (Hezser 2005: 69–82, 2019). Both slaves and wives lacked blood ties to the *ba'al ha-bayit* and entered the household from outside, through his "acquisition" of them (Ilan 1995: 88–89 for rabbinic texts; Ali 2010: 52 for early Islam). Therefore, they remained potentially dangerous and were subjected to his control. Within the household and family, the roles and functions of wives and female slaves were, to some extent, overlapping (Labowitz 2009: 147–198; Hezser 2013). If the owner and husband was dissatisfied with them, he could unilaterally sell his slaves and divorce his wife. Female slaves were doubly challenged by their status as slaves and women. Due to the sexual exploitation they suffered, slave women were considered promiscuous by rabbis. Even after manumission, they could not marry their (former) masters in a halakhically sanctioned way (m. Yebam. 2:8, Hezser 2013: 312), although such unions are likely to have existed, especially in societies in which polygamy was legal.

In her intersectional investigation of gendered enslavement in early Christian discourse, Bjelland Kartzow (2018) explores the links between Jewish and Christian monotheism and masculinity. The tradents and editors of the Hebrew Bible and postbiblical Jewish and Christian texts were free male householders who presented humans' relationship to God from their own gendered perspective. While the male authors may have identified themselves as God's "slaves," they considered their wives their own subordinates, expected to obey their orders and demands (Ilan 1995: 122). Thus, the author of the Hellenistic Jewish novel *Joseph and Aseneth* has Aseneth pray to God: "Give me to him as a servant, so that I may wash his feet and serve him and be his slave for all the seasons of my life" (13.12, translation with Cook). According to the rabbinic Midrash Avot de Rabbi Nathan (B 42), husbands "rule" over their wives since the time of creation, that is, "the author of the *midrash* finds women's subordination to men in the cosmic order established by Creation itself" (Ilan 1995: 132). Similarly, the author of the pastoral epistle to Titus admonishes "young women to love their husbands, to love their children, to be sober-minded, chaste, workers at home, kind, being in subjection to their own husbands, that the word of God be not blasphemed" (2:4–5), just as he instructs "servants to be in subjection to their own masters, and to be well-pleasing to them in all things" (2:9).

Since women and slaves were considered subordinate primarily to their husbands and masters and obliged to follow these human masters' instructions even as far as religious practices were concerned, Cohen (2005: 130) asks whether women were even considered proper Israelites and Jews, that is, members of the covenant with God, in the patriarchal social context in which ancient Jewish writings emerged. If circumcision as the sign of the covenant with God and Torah study and observance as its fulfilment were male prerogatives, where does that leave Jewish women (Cohen 2005: 132)? Could manumitted and circumcised male slaves achieve a higher status in Jewish communities than freeborn married women? Was Jewish (and Christian) monotheism – including self-identification with the Exodus experience – primarily geared at free male householders, whereas married women and slaves were considered these men's helpmeets, who could be liberated from his authority by divorce and manumission, that is, the male householder's power to end the relationship only? Do the literary sources provide any traces of women's and slaves' own perspectives and perceptions of their religiosities? Since Jewish women and slaves appear in the ancient sources "as imagined, constructed, and classified by Jewish men" (Cohen 2005: xii), a critique of the free male perspective may be easier than a reconstruction of the experience of the male householder's dependents.

As Glancy (2011) has already pointed out in connection with Christianity, various moral and theological problems arise from these foundational religious texts' representations of slaves and slavery, both in the metaphorical and real-life sense. Some of the problems and inconsistencies may have been noticed by the ancient tradents and editors already, whereas others are based on contemporary concerns. Despite the abolishment of slavery in Europe and the US, servile relationships with power imbalances and legal inequality continue to exist in a variety of forms. If monotheism is incompatible with slavery on moral and theological grounds, a historical-critical reading of the ancient texts may support an egalitarian ethics in which socioeconomic and gender-related discrimination is unacceptable and all humans, irrespective of their social status, have only God as their "master." One may go one step further, though, and question the conceptual appropriateness of master–slave metaphors in religious and philosophical discourse. Just as feminist Bible criticism has challenged the image of God as male, social criticism may reject the "slave," "master," and "householder" metaphors as outdated and inappropriate remnants of ancient slave-holding societies.

1 No Other Masters: The Incompatibility of Being Jewish and a Slave

Ancient rabbis were keenly aware of the incompatibility between the idea of the Exodus as God's liberation of Israelites from Egypt and actual enslavement, which required slaves to obey a human master. According to the Tosefta, the piercing of a slave's ear, mentioned in Ex. 21:5–6 as a marker of a Hebrew slave's voluntary permanent enslavement ("If the slave should say: I have loved my master and my wife and my children, I do not want to go out free ... his master shall pierce his ear with an awl and he shall be his slave forever"), serves as a reminder of the religious transgression he committed by bonding himself to a human master rather than serving God:

> And it [Scripture] says: 'and his master shall pierce his ear with an awl' [Ex. 21:6] – And why is the ear pierced in contrast to all [other] parts [of the body]? Because it heard from Mount Sinai: 'For unto me the children of Israel are slaves' [Lev. 25:55], [yet] it broke off the yoke of heaven and accepted upon itself the yoke of flesh and blood. Therefore Scripture says: Let the ear come and be pierced, because it did not observe what it heard. (t. B.Q. 7:5)

Being enslaved to a human master is not only considered incompatible with being a Jew but also declared a transgression and negation of the Exodus experience of divine redemption here. The "yoke of heaven," that is, having God as one's master, cannot be combined with enslavement to a human master. Jewish monotheism as redemption from slavery and Jews' enslavement in the real world are contradictory states that negate each other.

The biblical context of Ex. 21:6 refers to a male Hebrew slave's voluntary surrender to his Israelite master to be able to stay together in the same household with his servile family rather than be manumitted in the seventh year and separated from them (see the rule in Ex. 21:2). The context specifies that if the slave entered the household with his family, they should be released together; if he was given a wife by his master for purposes of procreation, to increase the number of slaves within the household, his wife and children remain enslaved when the Hebrew slave is released in the Sabbatical Year (Ex. 21:3–4). These specific circumstances are hardly envisioned by the Tosefta. Rather, the incompatibility between enslavement to a human master and having God as one's only master is stated in more general terms here.

In the Talmud Yerushalmi's parallel (y. Qid. 1:2, 59d) the connection to the Exodus experience is expanded in several regards. The Mishnah (m. Qid. 1:1–2) specifies the ways in which women and Hebrew slaves are "acquired" by the Jewish householder and ways in which they "acquire themselves," that is, are released from his authority over them. In both cases, money and a deed are means to "purchase" wives and slaves. Whereas wives cannot leave their husbands on their own initiative and become free after his death or a divorce that he initiates, Hebrew slaves are supposed to be manumitted in the Sabbatical (seventh) or Jubilee (fiftieth) Year.

The mishnaic manumission rules for Hebrew slaves were Scripture-based ideals rather than accounts of actual practice. This is especially evident from the suggestion to release a Hebrew slave girl when there are signs of the onset of puberty. The rule was meant to avoid the girl's sexual exploitation but is unlikely to have been heeded by slave owners, since it would have severely limited the value and use of young female Hebrew slaves. Freeborn Jewish girls could become debt slaves if their father owed money or produce to a wealthy creditor. Such a situation is envisioned in a parable transmitted in Sifre Deuteronomy 26 (Fraade 1983: 266): When the creditor did not receive (a guarantee for) his payment in due time, "he entered the man's house and seized his sons and daughters and placed them on the auction block [to be sold as slaves]." Although a non-Jewish creditor ("king") may be envisioned here, both Jewish and non-Jewish creditors could enslave their debtors' family members at least until the debt was paid off by the work they did for them. Since the value of debt slaves' labor is never specified – in contrast to the salary that free laborers received – the determination of the end of their forced labor would have been at the discretion of their owners. Debt slavery and other temporary forms of slavery were prohibited in Roman law (Wiedemann 1981: 40; Hezser 2003: 141), but still practiced in the Middle East in late antiquity. Not only rabbis but also Philo, Josephus, and the gospels of the New Testament were familiar with the practice (Zeitlin 1962–3: 194–195; Rosenfeld & Perlmutter 2020: 135; Stoutjesdijk 2020).

The Mishnah (m. Qid. 1:2) further specifies that a Hebrew slave whose ear is pierced will be enslaved to his master until the Jubilee Year. In its expansion of associations to the Exodus narrative, the Talmud (y. Qid. 1:2, 59d) brings up the issue of the door or door post as the place where the piercing of the ear is supposed to take place (Ex. 21:6). This location reminded Palestinian rabbis of the Exodus story, where Moses instructs Israelites to place animal blood on the lintels and two side posts of the doors of their houses (Ex. 12:22–23) so that God would recognize them and "pass over" their houses when striking the Egyptians. According to a tannaitic tradition attributed to R. Eliezer b. Yaqob, "by means of the [blood on their] door they [Israelites] went forth from slavery to freedom."

In the Talmud (y. Qid. 1:2, 59d), the Tosefta's anonymous tradition about the incompatibility of enslavement and the Exodus experience (t. B.Q. 7:5) is presented as a conversation between R. Yohanan b. Zakkai and his disciples.

R. Yohanan's answer to his disciples' question about the ear emphasizes the slave's transgression of biblical monotheism:

[A] His disciples asked R. Yohanan b. Zakkai: Why does this slave have his ear pierced rather than any [other] part [of his body]?

[B] He said to them: The ear which heard from Mount Sinai: 'You shall not have other gods besides me' [Ex. 20:3] and broke off the yoke of the kingdom of heaven and accepted upon itself the yoke of flesh and blood.

[C] The ear which heard before Mount Sinai: 'For unto me the children of Israel are slaves' [Lev. 25:55], and he went and acquired another master.

[D] Therefore, let the ear come and be pierced, because it did not observe what it heard.

R. Yohanan b. Zakkai's answer combines the first commandment of Jewish monotheism (Ex. 20:3) with the notion of God as one's only master (Lev. 25:55) to emphasize the incompatibility between a servile status, in which the authority of a human master reigns supreme, and a Jew's metaphorical enslavement to God. To willingly accept a servile status is presented as a grave sin and transgression here.

Slavery and Poverty

One may argue that no ancient Jew would have willingly succumbed to permanent slavery. Rather, a person would have been forced into slavery by his or her circumstances and persuaded to remain a slave by his or her master. With the exception of a few high-ranking and well-treated servile secretaries and businessmen in wealthy households, dire poverty and the inability to feed their children would have led Jews to consider self-sale, the sale of their children, debt slavery, and child abandonment as the last resorts to save their and their families' lives. Many Jewish families would have lost their landholdings as a consequence of the two unsuccessful revolts against Rome (Hamel 1990, 2010). Others had inherited tiny plots whose proceeds could not sustain large families. Droughts and bad harvests contributed to their plight. Thus, Hamel (2010: 309) writes: "[T]he limitations of food production meant that a substantial part of the population was at subsistence or poverty level and could easily lose the little security it had and fall into destitution."

Palestinian rabbis were aware of the difficult circumstances some of their fellow Jews found themselves in. They therefore made an exception to their general prohibition of self-sale and allowed a poor person to sell himself or herself to purchase cattle, utensils, or slaves for his or her family plot from the proceeds (t. Ar. 5:8). The text's parallel in Sifra (Behar 7:1, 80a) provides a biblical prooftext for the rule: "From where [do we know] that a person is not permitted to sell himself and to leave [the proceeds of the sale] in his money bag, or to purchase for himself utensils, or to purchase for himself a house, unless he is a poor person? Scripture says, 'And if he becomes poor and sells himself' [Lev. 25:39] – behold, he does not sell himself unless he is a poor person." According to the Mekhilta (Neziqin/Mishpatim 3), women are excluded from the permission to sell themselves as slaves, probably because it would have involved prostitution. The Tosefta emphasizes that male Jews' self-sale is a valid transaction and perhaps even permanent: "and if he sold [himself], behold, this one is sold" (t. Ar. 5:8). Since the money he received for the sale would henceforth support his family, there was little chance that he would ever acquire additional money to redeem himself. Manumission by his master remained an option, of course.

Did the rabbinic notion of the incompatibility between slavery and Jewishness apply to Jews whose poverty compelled them to sell themselves, who became the slaves of their creditors or were captured and enslaved by Romans? Several aspects have to be considered here: whether temporary enslavement could be considered a transient state at whose end full restitution to one's former status was possible; whether and to what extent Jewish and non-Jewish masters allowed their slaves to practice their native religion; and whether the circumstances of the slave's life and labor enabled him or her to observe Torah law and rabbinic rules. Could the slave maintain his or her Jewishness during enslavement or was this time an intermission from his or her former ethnic and religious status that could become permanent?

The Stigma Attached to Slavehood

Whereas status differences between freeborn Israelites and slaves are relatively blurred in the Hebrew Bible, where some of the patriarchs marry and have children and legitimate heirs with their female slaves (e.g., Gen. 16:3: Abraham and Hagar; Gen. 30:4: Jacob and Bilhah; Gen. 30:9: Jacob and Zilpah), in rabbinic sources a clear distinction is drawn between free Israelite and slave status. Rabbis devised rules that define the boundaries between the two categories. In rabbinic documents, "slave" (*eved*) is a generic category that is distinct from and cannot overlap with "Israelite." Slaves are entirely absent from rabbinically defined social hierarchies of Jewish society. For example, in Mishnah Hor. 3:8 priests and Levites stand at the top of the hierarchy, followed by ordinary Israelites. Below them, various "deficient" groups distinguished from Israelites are listed, with the proselyte and freed slave at the very bottom of the hierarchy. This arrangement is decisive for rabbinic views of formerly

Jewish slaves. Once they have been manumitted, they are considered "deficient" Jews who cannot become full Israelites again, since the status of "freed
slave" (*eved meshohrer*) will define them forever. Whereas members of other
"deficient" groups, such as the *mamzer* (the offspring of a forbidden sexual
relationship), can improve their status through Torah scholarship (m. Hor. 3:8),
this is not an option for manumitted slaves. While the *eved meshohrer* mentioned here must be imagined as originally Jewish (otherwise, this category
would not be part of the rabbinic hierarchy at all), he or she cannot regain their
former status, despite their Jewish ethnicity and monotheistic practice. Whether
they were forcefully enslaved or sold themselves, and whether they had Jewish
or non-Jewish masters is not taken into consideration.

The Tosefta (t. Hor. 2:10) parallel explains why the proselyte's status is
higher than that of a manumitted Jewish slave:

> R. Shimon b. Eliezer says: Rightfully, the freed slave should precede the
> proselyte, for this one [the freed slave] grew up in holiness [*qedoshah*] but
> that one [the proselyte] did not grow up in holiness. But [the proselyte
> precedes the freed slave] because this one [the freed slave] is subject to
> a curse [*arur*], but that one [the proselyte] is not subject to a curse.

In this statement, growing up as a freeborn person in a Jewish family is
associated with "holiness," that is, monotheistic beliefs and the observance of
Jewish customs. By contrast, the slave stands under a curse from a religious
point of view, since his Torah observance is highly questionable. The former
status of "holiness" cannot be restituted after the slave's manumission. Rather,
the curse of enslavement endures and determines his status and reputation
within Jewish society. That the stigma attached to slavehood endured the actual
period of enslavement and also applied to the formerly Jewish slaves' future
descendants is expressed in the Talmud Yerushalmi: "Do not believe a slave
until sixteen generations" (y. Hor. 3:5, 38b).

The freed slave's status could be transmitted to their offspring. If a free
Jewish woman married a freed slave, their offspring would have the status of
a freed slave (t. Qid. 4:14). Whereas male freed slaves were allowed to marry
the daughters of priests, marriage to a priest was prohibited to freed slave
women (m. Bikk. 1:5, t. Qid. 5:3), probably because they were suspected of
prostitution and promiscuity. Explaining why freeborn Jews hesitate to marry
freed slave women, the Tosefta states: "the freed slave woman is [assumed to be
in the status of] one who has been freely available" (t. Hor. 2:11). Here the
double stigmatization of slave women is obvious: like male slaves they were
considered to be "cursed"; as easily exploitable women they were considered
sexually tainted. Therefore, their reintegration into Jewish society would have

been severely impeded. According to the rabbinic sources discussed here, even temporary enslavement led to a permanent change of one's social and religious status, which could not be regained after manumission, especially as far as female slaves were concerned.

Slaves and Religious Practice

The reason for this harsh and discriminatory treatment of individuals whose enslavement was usually involuntary is the slave's status as the personal property (chattel) of the owner in both rabbinic halakhah and Roman law (Hezser 2005: 63–68). This status did not only involve the slaves' lack of legal rights but also the assumption that they lacked personhood in the sense of a distinct ethnic and religious identity that their master would respect and support. Rather, slaves were seen as "blank slates" on which the masters inscribed their own identities and values. Even if the owners were Jewish and rabbinic, however, they did not enable their slaves to fully observe the Torah, since slaves were not "obliged" to do so.

This is evident from the stories about R. Gamliel and his slave Tabi, who is presented as an ideal slave to his master's liking, interested in rabbinic study and observance. Rather than sleeping in the *sukkah* (temporary hut) on Sukkot, as free Israelite males would, Tabi is said to have "slept under the bed" in the *sukkah* in which sages were staying. This prompted his master's appreciative comment: "Do you see Tabi, my slave? He is a disciple of a sage, so he knows that slaves are exempt from [keeping the commandment of dwelling in] the *sukkah*. That is why he is sleeping under the bed" (m. Suk. 2:1). Tabi's Jewish or gentile origin is never specified and was probably considered irrelevant, since halakhically only his servile status mattered. Rabbis' ambiguous attitude toward their slaves' Torah observance and their general opposition to it is also evident from another Tabi tradition that deals with his use of *tefillin* (phylacteries worn by Jewish men during prayer). According to y. Suk. 2:1, 52d, "the opinions of R. Gamliel are contradictory. For it has been taught: Tabi, the slave of R. Gamliel, would put on *tefillin* and sages did not protest against him [cf. y. Er. 10:1, 26a]. But here [in m. Suk. 2:1] they protested against him." That even preferential household slaves were primarily seen as chattel is evident from a story about R. Eliezer, whose female slave had died (y. Ber. 2:8, 5b). The rabbi allegedly refused to accept condolences on her behalf, arguing: "And have they not said: One does not accept condolences on behalf of slaves because slaves are like cattle? If one does not accept condolences on behalf of freedmen, all the more so [does one not accept condolences] on behalf of slaves. To one whose slave or animal has died one says: May God restore your loss!"

Jewish slaves of Roman masters would have lived in pagan household environments in which they were obliged to contribute to, if not participate in pagan religious rituals. As Geary & Hodkinson (2012: 12) have pointed out, "[i]n ancient Greece and Rome household slaves were formally part of the extended *oikos* or *familia* and played subordinate roles in its religious rituals." Their religious engagement in the public sphere outside of the household was less controlled but would have depended on the respective religious cults' acceptance of slave participants. Whether and to what extent late antique Palestinian synagogues, which stood outside of rabbinic control, would have welcomed slaves and freed slaves into their midst is uncertain. Local synagogue communities may have enabled (freed) slaves to participate in prayer services, especially if they were in a position to offer donations. Two Greek donors inscriptions discovered on the mosaic floor of the Hammat Tiberias synagogue commemorate a certain Severus, who is called "*threptos* of the very illustrious patriarchs" (Roth-Gerson 1987: nos. 16 and 18; Di Segni 1988: nos. 29 and 30). Severus may have been a foundling (*threptos*) who was raised as a child or, more likely, as a slave in the patriarchal household (Hezser 2005: 103–104). His donation indicates that he was wealthy. Whether he was formerly Jewish or non-Jewish, enslaved or free is not specified. Like the *familia Caesaris*, the emperor's slaves, the slaves of the patriarch may have enjoyed a preferential status and prestige among Palestinian Jews which, again, indicates the significance of the master's own social standing and religious practice for the social and religious identity of his slaves.

Slaves and Hybrid Identity

Inscriptions may also point to some Jewish slaves' attempts to maintain vestiges of their Jewish ethnic and religious identity after their enslavement and deportation to Roman Italy. Despite the "denationalization" of enslaved Jewish war captives owned by Roman masters (Hezser 2005: 27–54), which involved the loss of their original names and inability to choose their sexual partners, the slaves would have remembered their ethnic and religious origins. In a few cases (the relatives of), those who were manumitted chose to express their geographical origins from Jerusalem and Judaea in public epitaphs. For example, a Latin inscription possibly from Naples set up by an imperial freedman commemorates "Claudia Aster, prisoner from Jerusalem" (Noy 1993: no. 26). If the imperial freedman Tiberius Claudius Proculus was pagan and her former owner and husband, as Noy assumes, she would hardly have maintained her Jewish religious identity but lived in a pagan household in Roman Italy until her death. The reference to Jerusalem serves as a reminder of her ethnic identity here. This is also the case in another inscription from third-century Ostia, in which the Jewish freedman Marcus Aurelius Pylades and his father Juda from Judaea are mentioned (Noy 1993: no. 15). The deceased is described as "the first pantomime of his time," honored by the order of the Augustales. Like Claudia Aster, he seems to have had a wealthy and prominent pagan Roman master and was probably well assimilated to Roman culture. While his family descent and ethnicity remained important to him, his religious identity may have been hybrid and syncretistic.

The inscriptions suggest that the time spent in the householder's cultural and religious realm became crucial for the slave's identity and remained decisive after manumission, especially if he or she was enslaved for a long time and linked to the master through (adopted) parentage or marriage ties. As a member of the Jewish patriarch's household Severus (mentioned above in the section on "Slaves and Religious Practice"), perhaps from a pagan background, decided to make a large donation to the local synagogue that he frequented. A freedwoman by the name of Calliope is commemorated in a Greek inscription in catacomb 20 at Bet She'arim (Schwabe & Lifshitz 1974: no. 200; CIJ no. 7196). She is introduced as "the freedwoman of Procopius, of illustrious memory," who, during her lifetime, held a high position (*mizotera*) in his household. The fact that she was buried in a Jewish cemetery suggests a certain affiliation with Judaism. As Rajak (2000: 492) has already pointed out, neither her and her owner's Greek names nor her status as a freedwoman necessitate the assumption of a Diaspora origin. Calliope probably played an important role in a wealthy Hellenised Jew's household and was considered sufficiently Jewish to be buried in a Jewish cemetery. By contrast, the formerly Jewish and Judaean slaves Claudia Aster and Marcus Aurelius Pylades seem to have been acculturated to the Roman environment of their owners and continued to live in such a context until their death.

The hypothesis that a slave's socialization in his or her master's household determined their religious affiliation more than their descent is also supported by Christian evidence. The book of Acts and the letters of Paul already mention that entire households were converted to Christianity and baptized when the householder decided to become Christian. Thus, Sandnes (1997: 152) writes: "The starting point of the churches was usually the conversion of the *pater-familias*, who embraced the Christian faith together with his whole household." The household included all of his dependents, that is, his wife and children as well as his slaves (e.g., Acts 16:5: Lydia of Thyatira and her household; cf. Acts 16:31–34 on the procedure). The conversion was not the dependents' decision and not based on their beliefs but forced upon them as members of a newly Christian master's household. Accordingly, Glancy (2002: 47) writes "that household baptisms masterminded by slaveholders raise uncomfortable questions about the social dynamics within the Pauline churches." Christian monotheism and its rituals were forced upon slaves from pagan (and Jewish) backgrounds by their master's use of power over them. While some of these baptized slaves may have aspired to be recognized as members of Christian communities, others probably developed hybrid identities that combined traces of their religious and cultural origins with their master's cultural and religious affiliations. Religious hybridity as a consequence of Christian religious hegemony has also been recognized for slaves of African descent in modern Western societies (Gerbner 2018: 9–18).

In early Byzantine times, when Christians had obtained political power, church leaders were concerned that (Christian) slaves in Jewish households might become Jewish. Whereas earlier rules prohibited Jews from circumcising their male slaves (Cod. Theod. 19.9.1 = Const. Sirm. 4: Constantine in 336 CE), later decrees prohibited the Jewish ownership of slaves altogether (Cod. Theod. 3.1–5, Gratian, Valentinian II, and Theodosius I in 384 CE). Whereas the earlier decree mentions both Christian slaves and slaves "of any other sect," the later rule is specifically targeted at the potential conversion of Christians to Judaism: "No Jew whatsoever shall purchase a Christian slave or contaminate an ex-Christian with Jewish religious rites." If "ex-Christian Jews" are found in Jewish households, these slaves will be declared free and their owners will be punished. Irrespective of whether and to what extent these rules were enforced, they are evidence of late antique Christian authorities' fears about imagined forced conversions of Christian slaves by Jewish owners (Hezser 2022: 135–136). Some of these "Christian" and "ex-Christian" slaves were probably slaves who had belonged to Christian owners who had forcefully converted them to Christianity before selling them to Jewish householders. Whereas the earlier decree seems to erroneously identify circumcision with conversion (see the considerations in the section on "Slavery in the Bible and Modern Abolitionism"), the later rule is more cognizant of the effects of slaves' religious socialization and adaptation to the cultural and religious identities of their owners.

Do these sources suggest that Jewish and Christian monotheism and enslavement were compatible, after all? Should we assume that baptized slaves in Christian households and circumcised and immersed slaves in Jewish households were able to more or less willingly practice the religions they were introduced to by their owners? This would have depended on the slaves' individual circumstances and roles within the household and on the attitudes of their masters. In general, slaves had a subservient status that required them to provide material support to their owners' religious practices rather than participating in them themselves. As we have already seen in connection with R. Gamliel's slave Tabi, slaves were not halakhically obliged to observe Torah rules that applied to free male Israelites and may have been prohibited from doing so to maintain clear-cut distinctions between the two social categories. Although the Torah rules that circumcised slaves may eat from the Passover sacrifice as members of Israelite households (Ex. 12:44) and the Mishnah and Tosefta include slaves (and women and minors) in the mixed *havurah* (table fellowship) gathered for the Passover meal (m. Pes. 8:7; t. Pes. 8:6), in reality only exceptionally valued household slaves are likely to have received this honor, while lower-ranking slaves would have performed the table service, delivering food and drink. We have to assume that during their time of enslavement slaves were rarely able to practice the religion/s of their choice. Those who were manumitted may have been welcomed only if they were wealthy male donors (synagogues) or committed to Torah study (rabbis), but there is little evidence to confirm this assumption.

2 The Humanity of Slaves: Master–Slave Relationships

According to Gen. 1:26, humans are created in God's "image" (*zelem*) and "likeness" (*demut*) and this notion is repeated in the next verse: "And God created the human being (*adam*) in His own image (*bezalmo*), in the image of God (*bezelem Elohim*) He created him; male and female He created them" (1:27). The verses emphasize that all human beings, irrespective of their gender and social status, are created in the image of God and therefore valued above all other created things. They possess a certain dignity and must be viewed accordingly. This notion has consequences for humans' treatment of other human beings. Already in Gen. 9:6 the injuring and killing of others is prohibited and must be severely punished: "He who sheds the blood of a human being, by a human being shall his blood be shed, for He made the human being in the image of God [*bezelem Elohim*]."

Slaves and Animals

The belief that human beings are created in God's image meant that they were distinguished from animals *qua* being human. Therefore, ancient Jews were strictly opposed to equating slaves to animals (Hezser 2005: 55–63), a notion that was commonly expressed in Greek and Roman philosophical texts. Aristotle already classified slaves together with household animals (Garnsey 1996: 110; Forsdyke 2021: 29), denying them the capacity to think rationally (*logos*) and to distinguish between right and wrong, which are characteristics of human nature in contrast to animals (Politics 1253a). The distinction between justice and injustice did not apply to slaves, since they were merely considered part of a householder's property, "for there is no such thing as injustice in the absolute sense toward what is one's own" (Aristotle, Nicomachean Ethics 5.6). As Garnsey (1996: 110) has pointed out: "For the author of the *Ethics* it would seem that 'slavery as such' is a less than human condition." The situation is not much different in Aristotles' *Politics*, where he specifies: "The slave is not merely the slave of the master but wholly belongs to the master" (1.1254a). As an "article of property," the slave can be used as an "instrument of action": Both slaves and animals "are essentially engaged in bodily service to secure the necessities of life for others" (Garnsey 1996: 112, with reference to Aristotle, Politics 1254b). Aristotles' animalization of slaves was not merely a personal conviction. Bradley (2000: 110) stresses that "the ease of association between slave and animal ... was a staple aspect of ancient mentality." Unfortunately, this view has endured in western culture for centuries and is still evident, for example, in the depiction of enslaved Black Africans in modern European and American literature and art (Pasierowska 2021: 40).

In his *Politics*, Aristotle moves from the equation between slaves and animals to the natural slave theory (Dobbs 1994; Pellegrin 2013), arguing that some people are born to be slaves, their bodies being different from those of free people: "The intention of nature therefore is to make the bodies also of freemen and of slaves different – the latter strong for necessary service, the former erect and unserviceable for such occupations, but serviceable for a life of citizenship" (1254b). The theory serves to legitimize slavery as natural and just: "It is manifest therefore that there are cases of people of whom some are freemen and the others slaves by nature, and for these slavery is an institution both expedient and just" (1255a).

The Natural Slave Theory and Imperialism

When applied to specific ethnic groups to justify their capture and enslavement in war, the theory can obtain (proto-)racist and imperialist connotations, as Isaac (2004: 505–506) has already pointed out: "The usual method of acquiring slaves is war ... war is therefore a legitimate process aimed at reducing inferior foreigners to the state of slavery for which nature has designed them anyway." When the Roman army conquered Jerusalem and captured and enslaved tens of thousands of Jews, Jews were seen as a "servile nation" justly subjected to Rome. Cicero, for example, called "the Jews and Syrians, nations born for slavery [*nationibus natis servituti*]" (On the Consular Provinces 5.10). The first-century Jewish historian Flavius Josephus seems to have been aware of this attitude (Hezser 2005: 61–62). Roman imperial conquests were the main basis

of Roman mass slavery, and the enslavement of parts of the conquered populations were justified by claims to their "natural" submission and inferiority
(Kahlos 2022: 93).

Ancient Jewish authors generally dismiss the Graeco-Roman equation of
slaves and animals and the natural slave theory. Based on the biblical creation
story, the Jewish philosopher Philo of Alexandria (first c. BCE to first c. CE)
argues for a hierarchy in creation, from the lowest types of animals to humans.
In his treatise he writes: "When the Creator determined to make animals, the
first created in his arrangement were in some degree inferior, such as the fishes,
and the last were the best, namely, man" (22:68). Philo considered humans the
most developed kind of animals because they possess reason. For him, the
creation of humans in the image of God referred to human intellectual capacity
(8.31). As humans, slaves possess reason, in contrast to "unreasoning animals."
Therefore the natural slave theory, which distinguishes between naturally
superior and inferior humans, is wrong:

> But the holiday of the Sabbath is given by the law not only to servants but also
> to the cattle, though there might well be a distinction. For servants are free by
> nature, no man being naturally a slave, but the unreasoning animals are
> intended to be ready for the use and service of men and therefore rank as
> slaves. (Special Laws 2.69; translation with Yonge)

Both animals and slaves are God's creatures and as such deserve a day of rest.
At the same time, Philo differentiates between slaves as humans, who possess
reason, and animals, who are said to lack that capacity (on this distinction
between humans and animals see Niehoff 2018: 70–73). Aristotles' distinction
between free humans and slaves is shifted to slaves (as human beings) and
animals here. At the same time the Aristotelean idea that some people are born
to slavehood is explicitly dismissed: No human being is natually a slave (see
also Garnsey 1994: 35). Rather, one may become a slave through unfortunate
political and socioeconomic circumstances. Although Philo also uses the term
"slave" metaphorically for someone who is "enslaved" to emotions and desires,
in this text he refers to physical slavery and the labor associated with it.

In another text Philo criticizes the enslavement of freeborn persons and
praises masters who emancipate their slaves:

> [M]an, as it seems, has been assigned the most preeminent position among the
> animals, being, as it were, a near relation of God himself, and akin to him in
> respect of his participation in reason ... On which account everyone who
> feels any admiration of virtue is full of exceeding anger, and is utterly
> implacable against kidnappers, who for the sake of most iniquitous gain
> dare to inflict slavery on those who are free by birth, and who partake of

the same nature as themselves. For if masters perform a praiseworthy action when they emancipate slaves born in their house or purchased with money, even though they have often not done them any great service, from the slavery in which they are held, because of their own humanity by which they are influenced, how heavy ought to be the accusation which is brought against those who deprive of that most excellent of all possessions, freedom, those who are at present in possession of it; when it is an object for which man, who has been well born and properly brought up, would think it glorious to die? (Special Laws 4.14–15; translation with Yonge)

Philo's disapproval is directed against kidnappers here, who capture and sell freeborn individuals and "bring slavery not only upon strangers and foreigners, but even upon those of the same nation as themselves" (4.16). In support of his criticism he invokes the biblical notion of humans as reasonable beings created in the image of God. This essence of being human does not end with enslavement but applies to slaves as human beings. It makes all forms of slavery, including homeborn and purchased slaves, problematic and their manumission praiseworthy. Although Philo does not call for the abolishment of the institution of slavery as such, he considers slavery problematic and difficult to reconcile with biblical anthropology. Since humans are "like" God, only freedom can be their proper state.

Elsewhere, Philo praises the Essenes, who do not own slaves and consider slavery "contrary to nature," since "nature has created all men free" (De Vita Contemplativa 9.70). The enslavement of other humans is caused by "the injustice and covetousness of some men who prefer inequality, that cause of all evil," and exploit those who are weaker than themselves (Philo, De Vita Contemplativa 9.70). Among the Essenes, the younger "free men minister to the guests, performing the offices of servants" voluntarily (Philo, De Vita Contemplativa 9.70; Ramelli 2016: 89). An analogy to this phenomenon existed in later rabbinic circles, where freeborn students are expected to "serve" their masters (*shimush hakhamim*) at table and in other daily tasks (Hezser 2005: 174–178). Another group spotlighted by Philo are the Therapeutai, ascetics about whom little is known. According to Philo, they "worship" animals and slaves as creatures at the bottom of the social hierarchy (De Vita Contemplativa 1.9).

Philo's criticized slave practices as a wealthy Jewish aristocrat in Roman Egypt. His criticism is based on both the Greek Bible with its view of humans as superior to animals, God-like and free, and on Stoic ideas. According to Colish (1985: 37), "the Stoics argue that slavery and sexual inequality are contrary to the law of nature. The Stoics' critique of slavery is consistent throughout the history of the school. Some Stoics who owned slaves manumitted them. At the same time, the Stoics do not expressly demand the abolition of slavery as a social institution" but emphasize "the duty to recognize the moral dignity of slaves and to treat them humanely." As members of the urban elite, Philo and Stoic philosophers probably owned slaves themselves (cf. Special Laws 2.123, where Philo calls slaves "indispensable property," whose services are required in daily life; on Stoic slave ownership, see Ramelli 2016), but their religious and philosophical values would have motivated them to treat them with dignity and kindness.

Esau, Ham, and "Natural" Slavery

Does Philo consider the biblical Ham and Esau "natural slaves," as Garnsey (1994: 37) has argued, and therefore resemble Aristotle more than his criticism of natural slavery may suggest? The biblical story about the brothers Jacob and Esau is often invoked in modern discussions about slavery, nationalism, and anti-Semitism (Lindemann 1997: 3–6; Hacohen 2019: 55–136). According to the biblical narrative, Isaac's wife Rebecca gave birth to twin brothers, Jacob and Esau, who are called the ancestors of "two nations" (Gen. 25:23). The phrase, "two nations are in your womb" has become a catchphrase in modern scholarship, which is applied to relations between Jews and Christians (Yuval 2008), Jews and Arabs (Kasher 1988: 25–26), or Jews and non-Jewish "Others" with variant meanings in the different time periods and contexts in which the terminology was used (Bakhos 2006: 23–30 and 2007; Langer 2010; Aminof 2015). After Jacob had convinced Esau to sell his birthright to him (Gen. 25:33), Isaac expresses Esau's relationship to Jacob with the words: "I have made him master [*gvir*] over you, and all his brothers I have given him as slaves [*avadim*]" (Gen. 27:36). The servile language is used here to express Jacob's superiority as the now recognized firstborn son. In the reconciliation scene in Gen. 32–33, it is Jacob who identifies himself as Esau's "slave." While the family is said to have owned real slaves, who are mentioned throughout the narrative, the terms are clearly used figuratively here (Bridge 2014).

Another case in point is Ham, one of Noah's sons (Gen. 6:10) and the father of Canaan (9:18, 22). As a punishment for having seen his father naked and not covered him up, the offspring of Ham is cursed by Noah in Gen. 9:25: "Cursed be Canaan. He shall be a slave of slaves [*eved avadim*] to his bothers" (see also Gen. 9:26–27). In later interpretations, Ham has been identified with Black Africans and the biblical tradition "has been the single greatest justification for Black slavery for more than a thousand years" (Goldenberg 2003: 1). Goldenberg shows that in the Bible Ham is not associated with blackness and his name received this connotation in later interpretations only: "We first see this kind of explicit link between skin color and slavery in Near Eastern sources beginning in the seventh century" (Goldenberg 2003: 170). The ways in which the biblical texts, foremost among them Genesis 9, have been misused in modern times to justify discrimination, racial segregation, and slavery are explicated by Whitford (2016).

Does Philo use the texts about Esau and Ham in the sense of Aristotle's natural slave theory, that is, does he suggest that the descendants of Esau and Ham were born to be slaves in the physical sense of the term and subservient to the Israelite/Jewish "nation"? In his treatise *Every Good Man Is Free*, Philo alludes to the biblical Esau story without explicitly mentioning Jacob's and Esau's names:

> [I]n a case where there were two brothers, the one temperate and the other intemperate, the common father of them both, taking pity on the intemperate one who did not walk in the path of virtue, prays that he may serve his brother, conceiving that service which appears in general to be the greatest of evils is the most perfect good to a foolish man, in order that thus he may be deprived of his independence of action, so as to be prevented from misconducting himself with impunity, and that he may be improved in his disposition by the superintending management of him who is appointed to be his master. (8.57; translated with Yonge)

Crucial for a proper understanding of the passage is the distinction between a literal and figurative use of the slave–master terminology. Philo declares physical slavery "the greatest of evils" here. Rather than associating slavery with any particular group or "nation," the terminology is used figuratively to express the benefits of the instructions of "the wise," that is, (religious) philosophers and intellectuals, over those whose might need their guidance in their lives. The latter are encouraged to accept "the wise" as "masters" over themselves to improve their conduct. In the literary context Philo associates his biblical interpretation with the Stoic philosopher Zeno's question: "Shall not the wicked man suffer if he contradicts the virtuous man?" (8.53), suggesting that "Zeno appears to have drawn this maxim of his as it were from the fountain of the legislation of the Jews" (8.57). Clearly, the idea that philosophical virtue should guide the "wicked" is at issue here.

In his treatise *On Sobriety*, Philo provides an allegorical interpretation of the biblical story about Noah's drunkenness and the curse of Canaan. Again, his real topic is the relationship between "the wise" and "foolish," that is, between philosophers and the unlearned masses. Philo rejects a literal interpretation of the text, which may not answer the question why Canaan rather than Ham is cursed (7.33). "Ham" rather stands for "wickedness in a state of inactivity," while "Canaan" represents "wickedness in a state of motion" (10.44).

Accordingly, Noah has "assigned the fool to be a slave to those who cultivate virtue, that, either by passing under a better government he may live a better life, or if he continue in evil doing he may easily be punished by the independent authority of his masters" (13.69). The allegorical interpretation of the Ham episode is very similar to that of the Esau story, namely, that the "wise" should rule over the "foolish," philosophers over the unlearned masses. None of these texts condemns a certain set of people to "natural slavery." If the masses follow philosophers' instructions, they will be considered "wise" themselves.

Garnsey is therefore wrong in claiming that Philo "is quite specific about the existence of a class of natural slaves" (Garnsey 1994: 37). As already shown, Philo interprets the biblical texts about Esau and Ham allegorically and uses the slavery terminology figuratively rather than referring to "acts of physical enslavement" (Garnsey 1994: 37), which are not mentioned in the Bible either. This is also the case in his *Allegorical Interpretation*, as the name of the tractate already indicates. In Philo's exegesis the "two nations" of Gen. 25:23 are neither associated with a particular people or ethnic group nor with physical slavery. Rather, Jacob the "despot" (*despotes*) and "master" stands for reason and all actions based on it, whereas Esau the "slave" stands for un-reason or irrationality and its consequences (3.19.88–89). His view of "natural slavery" is expressed as follows: "For that which is bad [*phaulon*] and unreasonable [*alogon*] is, by nature [*physei*], a slave before God; but that which is good and reasonable ... is powerful and free before him" (3.19.89).

Philo interprets the Bible from a Hellenistic philosophical point of view and reflects the philosophical notion of philosophers' and their students' and followers' superiority over the unlearned masses. Like Philo, Stoics expected their contemporaries to be "reasonable enough to recognize the superiority of the wise who, for this reason, will also be kings" (Frede 1978: 69). As Garnsey himself has pointed out elsewhere (1996: 138), the Stoics viewed the relationship between the wise and their "inferiors" in terms of the master–slave relationship. They considered real slaves to possess reason and the ability to strive for virtue. The distinction between wisdom and foolishness was therefore not linked to real-life enslavement and freeborn status. The Stoic approach, which reasoned "that legal slavery was an external condition over which one had no control," was contrary to Aristotle's natural slave theory, as Owens (2022: 12) has pointed out. Philo's exegesis must be viewed within this Stoic philosophical context to be understood properly.

Ethical Recommendations for the Treatment of Slaves

As far as physical slavery is concerned, Philo advises slave owners to treat their slaves mildly, but this concern primarily applies to Jews who were reduced to slavery through unfortunate circumstances. In the *Special Laws* he comments on the biblical rule to release Hebrew slaves in the seventh year of their service (2.18.79). Jewish masters should consider their Jewish slaves relatives of the same family, tribe, and nation whose destitute circumstances caused their current state (2.18.82). They deserve "proper relaxation and well-regulated periods of rest" (2.18.83). In the seventh year "let him who is free by nature depart in freedom" (2.18.84). Philo alludes to the biblical law about the inclusion of slaves and cattle in Sabbath rest (Ex. 23:12): If the earth is allowed to rest, how much more should human beings enjoy a period of relaxation, given that they possess reason and can feel pain (2.19.89). The statement "Cease, therefore, you who are called masters, from imposing harsh and intolerable commands on your slaves, which break the strength of the body by their compulsion, and compel the soul to faint even before the bodies" (2.19.90) resembles the advice given to masters by Roman agricultural writers such as Cato and Columella, who advocated rest and nourishment to increase slaves' productivity (Westermann 1955: 76).

Philo considers the continuous possession of non-Jewish slaves legitimate, necessary, and justified on the basis of Scripture: "But the law permits the people to acquire a property in slaves who are not of their own countrymen, but who are of different nations ... for there are an innumerable host of circumstances in life which require the ministrations of servants" (Special Laws 2.25.123). The biblical distinction between Hebrew and Canaanite slaves is upheld here and applied to formerly Jewish and non-Jewish slaves of Philo's own time. Such slaves may be punished, so that they fear their master and refrain from disobeying him (On the Giants 11.46). The commitment of physical injuries is criticized, though. If a master has knocked out his slave's eye, the slave shall be set free (cf. Ex. 21:26), "for thus he will suffer a double punishment for the actions which he has committed, in being deprived of the value of his slave and of his services" preventing him from further mistreatment of his slaves (Allegorical Interpretation 3.35.196–197). Furthermore, "the law also commands that if any one strike out the tooth of a slave he shall bestow his freedom on the slave" (Allegorical Interpretation 3.36.198 referring to Ex. 21:27). Philo explains that teeth are an important part of the body, necessary for the intake of food, thus enabling life which "is a thing of great value." Philo uses biblical law to warn masters against misusing their authority over slaves here. Such behavior will backfire and result in the master's own loss.

Later rabbinic rules about the treatment of slaves, transmitted between c. 70 CE and 350 CE, are based on the same biblical foundation and must also be understood in the context of Roman law and Graeco-Roman philosophy. For example, a story about R. Gamliel and his slave Tabi relates that "R. Gamliel knocked out the tooth of his slave Tabi" to set him free (y. Ket. 3:10, 28a par. y. Shevu.5:7, 36 c). While the biblical law (Ex. 21:27) considers manumission the morally correct punishment of a master who mistreats his slave, in the Talmud R. Yehoshua states: "It is not in your power [to set him free] and there are no fines except [in cases involving] witnesses and a court" (y. Ket. 3:10, 28a). If R. Gamliel wanted to manumit his slave, he could have done so without knocking out his tooth, namely, by giving him a writ of manumission. For the action to be a valid basis for manumission, the master's simple self-declaration is insufficient. Rather, witnesses and a court hearing are required to verify the deed. The story is transmitted as an illustration of the "general principle" mentioned at the end of Mishnah Ketubot 3:10 here: "Whoever pays more [compensation] than the damage he has done, he does not [have to] pay on the basis of his own [testimony]." Rather, additional witnesses are necessary and the compensation should be determined by the court. Since manumission was deemed a punishment that was out of proportion of R. Gamliel/the master's treatment of his slave, R. Yehoshua considered the legal process mandatory.

The text suggests that in rabbinic times a master's mistreatment of his slave did not lead to automatic manumission. In general, a master's physical punishment of his slave was considered a common aspect of the master–slave relationship (Hezser 2005: 204–211). Lewis (2018: 40) points to "the near total lack of restrictions on mistreatment of slaves" in Greek society: "Masters could corporally punish their slaves in whatever manner they deemed fit," since the matter was considered a private affair rather than being governed by public legislation. In Roman law, masters had the power of life and death over their own slaves (Garnsey 1996: 26), which means that they could inflict a punishment that led to their death. As Buckland (1970: 434) has pointed out, "[a] slave is a mere nullity at civil and praetorian law. He has no *caput*, or what seems to be the same thing, his *caput* has no *ius*." Slaves had no legal means to sue their masters. On the other hand, some Roman emperors tried to prevent overt cruelty against slaves (Harris 2001: 329–332; Hezser 2005: 205–206) and some Graeco-Roman philosophers appealed to slave owners to control their anger (Harris 2001: 88–126).

The Shared Humanity of Slaves and Free People

In fact, Seneca's admonition to show kindness to slaves seems to be based on a similar notion as the biblical idea that all humans were created equal (Gen. 1:27: creation "in the image of God"; Gen. 2:7: "breath of life," "living soul"). According to Seneca, slaves "rose from the same seed to enjoy the same sky, to breathe the same, to live the same, to die the same" as other human beings

(Epistles 47.10: *ex isdem seminibus ortum eodem frui caelo, aeque spirare, aeque vivere, aeque mori*). All human beings, irrespective of their enslavement or freedom, have "the same origins" (On Benefits 3.28.1: *Eadem omnibus principia eademque origo*). According to Hunt (2018: 199), "[t]his refers to the Stoic belief that the same divine spirit – *pneuma*, literally 'breath' – constitutes the soul of all people (*Epistles* 31.11). All souls have this same origin and composition and all humans share a sort of kinship." The connection between this belief and Stoic recommendations for the mild treatment of slaves are obvious: "From this fellowship of all humanity, Seneca infers that we have a duty to be kind to slaves" (Hunt 2018: 199).

As an example for such kindness, both Seneca and the rabbis refer to the provision of the same food that their masters eat, but they are also aware of the exceptionality of this practice. Seneca recommends masters to eat at the same table with the slaves they value most: "Shall I bring all slaves to my table? . . . I will not judge them by their services but by their character . . . Some will dine with you because they are worthy (*Quidam cenent tecum, quia digni sunt*)" (Epistles 47.15). The preferential treatment of "worthy" slaves has an analogy in rabbinic texts. In fact, the same explanation is used in a story about R. Gamliel and his slave Tabi in the Mishnah (m. Ber. 2:7). To justify his acceptance of condolences on the occasion of his slave Tabi's death, R. Gamliel tells his students that "is not like the rest of slaves, he was worthy [*kosher*]." Several further examples of exceptional slaves are transmitted in rabbinic literary sources (Hezser 2005: 157–162).

The offer of better food than is customary for slaves is associated with R. Yohanan: "Now did not R. Yohanan, from whatever he would eat, give to his slave and recite the following verse in this connection: 'Did not he who made me in the womb make him' [Job. 31:15]" (y. Ket. 5:5, 30a). Whether a joint meal is envisaged here remains uncertain. Household slaves – probably the most valued only – were supposed to be included in the table fellowship of the Passover *seder*, not only in the meal but also in the conversations (m. Pes. 8:7; t. Pes. 8:6). Similarly, Seneca suggests that the householder conducts conversations with his slaves: "Live with the slave mercifully, politely also, and admit him into conversation, both in advice and in living together [*Vive cum servo clementer, comiter quoque, et in sermonem illum admitte et in consilium et in convictum*]," being aware that some of his fellow slave owners would fiercely reject such a practice (Epistles 47.13).

The similarities between Seneca and the mentioned rabbinic traditions are striking. In the first four centuries CE, "wise men" of different backgrounds seem to have recommended a lenient treatment of slaves, based on their shared humanity, and given preferential treatment to those slaves they valued most, on the basis of their character and ability to join them in conversation. While biblical monotheism (rabbis) and Stoic philosophy (Seneca) would have played a role in reaching these positions, in all likelihood these scholars' own status and roles within their respective societies were decisive as well. As intellectuals they occupied a social position between the unlearned and illiterate freeborn masses and the landholding political and administrative elite. Although few if any rabbis would have matched Seneca's upper-class background and function as imperial advisor, both rabbis and Stoic philosophers represented values and followed practices that were distinct from those of the "unlearned" masses. Although they would have tried to persuade others to follow their example and advised them on daily life practice, it is impossible to say how influential they were beyond their circles of students and followers. As "wise men" they relied on instruction and persuasion rather than on official political or legal authority. Although rabbis devised numerous halakhic rules that concerned the proper treatment of slaves (Hezser 2003 and 2005), they could not force their rules on their contemporaries. Whether and to what extent rabbis' instructions and advice had an impact on their coreligionists beyond their own families, disciple circles, and sympathizers remains unknown.

Servile Submission as a Christian Religious Duty

Whereas Christian writers of the first four centuries CE functioned in a similar context, admonitions to slaveholders to treat their slaves mildly are replaced by advice to slaves to obey their masters in the name of Christianity. Glancy (2002: 140–141) has pointed out that "Paul himself speaks only obliquely of praise-worthy behavior for slaveholders, for example, instructing Philemon to regard Onesimus as a brother," yet "the letter does not comment on expectations or standards for the behavior of Christian slaveholders toward non-Christian slaves." In these regards, Paul resembles Philo of Alexandria, whose advice to slave owners primarily concerns the mild treatment of their enslaved Jewish "brothers" and "sisters," as already discussed. In contrast to Philo, Seneca, and the rabbis, however, who provided recommendations to slave owners, the Christian household codes (*Haustafeln*) of the late first and second centuries CE urge slaves in Christian households – who were forcefully baptized with their master – to show "[o]bedience, humility, industriousness, patience, self-effacement" (Glancy 2002: 140), that is, the common moral virtues that Graeco-Roman slave owners hoped to see in their slaves (see, for example, Col. 3:22–24). According to Glancy (2002: 141), they seem to simply express expectations of "normative behavior" in slave–master relationships. As far as slave owners are concerned, the author's instructions are very brief:

"Masters [*kyrioi*], treat your slaves justly and fairly, knowing that you also have a master [*kyrion*] in heaven" (4:1). Here the notion of God/Christ as one's master is extended backward so that a hierarchical structure emerges: Just as God is the master of the freeborn Christian slave owner, the latter is master over his slaves. At both stages justice should rule the master–slave relationship, but no further details or examples are given. Glancy (2002: 141) is correct in her observation that "the Colossians household code clearly casts the quotidian submission of slaves to their slaveholders as a Christian obligation."

The situation is similar in the Pastoral Epistles (1 and 2 Timothy and Titus), which were written at a time when Christianity tried to attract members of the upper strata of Graeco-Roman society. Rather than addressing slaveholders and admonishing them to treat their slaves well, these letters urge slaves to obey their masters and present this obedience as God-willed behavior. Thus, the author of 1 Timothy writes: "Let as many slaves as are under the yoke count their own masters [*despotas*] worthy of all honor, that the name of God and his doctrine be not blasphemed" (6:1). The slaves shall "not despise" their Christian masters but "do them service" (6:2). Similarly, the Letter to Titus insists: "Exhort slaves to be obedient unto their own masters, and to please them well in all things, not talking back ... that they may adorn the doctrine of God our savior in all things" (2:9–10). The reference to Christian beliefs serves to strengthen masters' power over their slaves here. As Glancy (2002: 145) succinctly puts it, these texts show that "the Roman Empire triumphs over the social values of Christianity." Later Christian slave owners, slave traders, and anti-abolitionists found support for their positions in these early Christian texts (Tise 1987: 117–118; Lowance 2003: 51–87).

3 Humans as Slaves of God: Slavery as Metaphor and Reality

As we have already seen, in the Hebrew Bible and in postbiblical Jewish literature, Israelites and Jews present themselves as the "slaves" of God and God as their "master." These slavery metaphors were also used in early Christianity (Martin 1990; Harris 1999; Byron 2003; Bjelland Kartzow 2018) and Islam (El-Sharif 2012; Sheikh 2019), where they were adapted to the respective beliefs and theological contexts. At the time when these texts were written, slavery was an ubiquitous and commonly accepted practice the tradents and editors would have been familiar with from the social environments they lived in, even if they were neither slaves nor slave owners themselves.

As literate scholars, the editors of the ancient Jewish, Christian, and Islamic compilations are unlikely to have experienced enslavement themselves. Whether they owned slaves is uncertain. As members of the upper strata of society, Philo and Josephus are likely to have owned a few household slaves, one of whom probably served as a scribe and secretary. Rabbis, on the other hand, mostly belonged to the so-called middling strata of society, that is, professionals (e.g., merchants and artisans) who worked for their own livelihood (Hezser 1997: 257–266) and neither needed nor could afford slaves. In Palestinian rabbinic literature only a few wealthy and prominent rabbis such as the patriarch are represented as slave owners (Hezser 2005: 294–298). Even if rabbis had never been slaves themselves and did not own slaves, they spoke and wrote from the perspective of free(born) male Jews who distinguished themselves from slaves as their social superiors. Tannaitic and amoraic traditions and rabbinic documents are addressed to other free male Jews, primarily fellow scholars. Rabbinic texts that mention slaves are therefore always formulated from the perspective of and addressed to the free adult male Jew. The phenomenon that rabbinic texts, in contrast to the Christian household codes and pastoral epistles, do not provide instructions for slaves can be explained by their intended audience of fellow-scholars rather than Jews in general or Jewish communities.

How could ancient intellectuals who were familiar with slavery, even if they were neither slaves nor slave owners themselves, see themselves as the "slaves" of God and how did they envision this relationship? What did they perceive as the shared parameters of slavery and a rabbinically defined Jewish religiosity that warranted the use of slavery metaphors? The most obvious notions are (1) the great hierarchical difference between God and humans; (2) God as the issuer of commandments and rules that humans must follow; (3) humans being punished by God physically, even unto death; and (4) the notion of God's ownership and control of humans. These beliefs are fundamental to biblical and rabbinic theology and religious practice. One may even argue that biblical monotheism is based on and perceived as a slave–master relationship that elevates slavery to the divine sphere. Ancient Israelites and Jews, as well as Christians and Muslims, considered slavery *the* – or at least one of the – most useful *Bildfeld* (field of images) to depict their relationship to God.

Other metaphors may have been considered less useful because they suggest a too great familiarity between God and humans (father, friend) or a too great leniency and *laissez faire* attitude on God's side (forgiveness, mercy, support), although these notions also appear in the literary sources and stand in a creative tension with the slave–master imagery. As far as the ancient texts are concerned, all of these images were created and used by men, that is, God and his relationship to humans is presented from a male perspective. This also applies to the slavery imagery: God is imagined as a male master and his self-perceived slaves are primarily male. Where this leaves wives – who, in the rabbinic male imagination, were seen as dependents of the householder in analogy to slaves – female slave owners, and female slaves in their relationship to the Divine remains unexplored as far as ancient Judaism is concerned (see Bjelland Karzow for an intersectional approach to slavery metaphors in early Christian texts).

The Hierarchical Difference between God and Humans

The first imagined similarity between God and a slave master is the great hierarchical distinction between God/master and humans/slaves, a theological belief that is evident in the Hebrew Bible already and continues in postbiblical perceptions of God. Just as human slave owners were the heads of their households, with (almost) absolute power over their dependents, God was imagined as vastly superior to humans, who were considered dependent on him in all aspects of their lives. In comparison to the householder, identified as a free male Israelite by rabbis, slaves were non-entities who did not even feature in the rabbinic hierarchical scheme until they were manumitted and placed at its very bottom (see m. Hor. 3:8). It is the superiority of the master over the slave and the slave's lowliness in comparison to his master that would have inspired ancient Israelites' and later Jews', Christians', and Muslims' self-identification as "slaves" of God. By declaring themselves the "slave" of God, free male Israelites and Jews expressed their religious humility in face of the Divine, even if they were high-standing individuals in real life.

In ancient Jewish literary sources the self-identification as a "slave" of God appears much more frequently than the use of the "master" metaphor for God. This suggests that the terminology was mainly used to express religious self-perception than to make a theological statement about God. Already in the Hebrew Bible the main context in which individuals call themselves God's slave is prayer. For example, in the scene that describes Abraham's hospitality toward the angels, Abraham prays to God and the angels as his representatives, asking for divine favor and support, by not only calling himself God's/the angels' "slave" (Gen. 18: 3, 5) but also offering to carry out servile tasks for them (fetching water to wash their feet, offering water and bread). Interestingly, the work itself is then delegated to his wife Sarah (18:6: baking bread) and a slave (*na'ar*, lit. "young man," in 18:7: preparing a calf to be cooked). Nevertheless, Abraham carries out the table service himself (18:8), probably because it involved direct contact with the angels and enabled him to show his humility in front of the Divine, whereas Sarah remains hidden in the tent for the entire duration of the meeting (18:9–10).

The biblical scene of hospitality to the angels is depicted visually in several early Byzantine churches, for example, as part of the Abraham cycle of wall mosaics in the sixth-century CE basilica of San Vitale in Ravenna (Jensen 2024: Figure 3.8). Here, the hospitality scene is depicted right next to the Binding of Isaac (Aqedah) scene within the same arch. In both scenes Abraham takes center stage and he is depicted in two guises: as a "slave" in a short garment carrying food to the angels' table on the left-hand side and as a patriarch in a *tallit* (prayer shawl) with stripes, who is about to fulfil God's commandment of "sacrificing" his son (on the Christian understanding of the Aqedah story see Hezser 2018: 53–60) on the right. Whereas the first embodiment of Abraham (hospitality scene) is that of a "real" slave of the Divine, in the second image (Aqedah) he represents a "slave in spirit" who does not hesitate to fulfil God's commandments, even if it means the loss of what is dearest to him. Jensen (2024, forthcoming) suggests that "[t]he story of Abraham's hospitality in this context could have resonated with the prayer spoken by the presider at the altar as he consecrated the elements in the eucharist ritual." In the Byzantine Christian theological context, Abraham "served" God by "sacrificing" his "son" and thereby bringing about salvation, an idea that found ritual expression in the eucharist.

In the San Vitale mosaic Sarah is shown in the left-hand corner behind Abraham, inside her house in the open door but not in the presence of the angels, which only Abraham is considered worthy of. Her presence is justified by her role as the target of the angels' prophecy and as Isaac's mother, but she is not depicted as a "slave" of God, an honor that is associated with the male householder and patriarch Abraham only. In the earlier fifth-century depiction of the hospitality scene in a wall mosaic of the basilica of Santa Maria Maggiore in Rome (Jensen 2024: Figure 3.7) Sarah is more visible in front of her house as the baker who prepares the bread for the angels. In this rendering, neither she not Abraham are depicted as "slaves," however, but don the clothes of burghers, Abraham – who seems to be depicted twice here, instructing Sarah and serving the angels – wearing a *tallit* like the one in the Aqedah scene in the basilica of San Vitale. In the context of the surrounding Christocentric wall mosaics, Abraham appears as an intermediary and witness of a divine prophecy which the viewers were invited to associate with "Christ's incarnation," that is, Christian theology was superimposed on the biblical narratives (Miles 1993: 159–160).

As far as the Hebrew Bible is concerned, the self-identification as a "slave" of God appears dozens of times in the book of Psalms. The reciter of the prayers addresses God directly, asking him to treat his "slave" in certain ways: for example, to keep him away from sin (Ps. 19:14), not to distance himself from his "slave" in anger (27:9), to be merciful to his "slave" (31:17), to enjoy the "wellbeing [*shalom*] of his slave" (35:27), to revenge the killing of his "slave" by other nations who do not worship the Israelite God (79:10), to give his strength to his "slave and salvation to the son of his maidservant" (86:16, cf. 116:16 for this expression). In the Psalms, God is indirectly presented as an ideal master, who treats his slaves mercifully and defends them against their enemies. Especially in connection with Abraham (105:6, 42), Moses (105:26), and David (78:70; 89:3, 20) as God's "slaves," the aspect of chosenness is evident: Just as the slave owner selects slaves for his household in accordance with the tasks they are supposed to fulfil and the loyalty he can expect of them, God has chosen his "slaves" from among the nations. As members of his "household" they stand under his protection. Female slaves are mentioned as the mothers of the "slaves" of God only. As other ancient Jewish texts, the Psalms are formulated from the perspective of the male worshiper, expressing male hopes of divine protection. A woman's self-identification as God's "maidservant" appears only later, in the Hellenistic novel Joseph and Aseneth (17:7), in Aseneth's prayer to God. At the same time, traditional household hierarchies remain in place, for Aseneth is also presented as her husband Joseph's slave (6.8, 13.12).

While Philo was aware of the theological use of the slave–master terminology in the Bible and subscribes to it to some extent, he also suggests alternative metaphors for the relationship between "the wise" and God. On the one hand, he claims that God as the master and ruler of the entire universe is vastly superior to "the so-called human masters," so that "in truth" humans have only one master, namely, God (On the Cherubim 25.83). Like Josephus (Ant. 16.156–157). Philo would have been aware and critical of Roman emperors' use of the master–slave terminology to urge their subjects into submission and deference to them. For Philo, to serve God is superior to freedom and other worldly goods (On the Cherubim 31.107). On the other hand, the masses are urged to become "slaves of the wise," accepting and following their guidance (Allegorical Interpretation 3.69.193) and the wise, with whom Philo obviously identified, should be seen as the "friends" of God rather than his servants: "for the wise is more a friend to God than a slave," presenting Abraham as an example (On Sobriety 11.55). While human piety can be considered "service" to God, Philo also notes that unlike human masters God does not need slave labor; therefore, as far as humans as the "slaves" of God are concerned, "to God they supply nothing beyond a mind imbued with a spirit of willing obedience" (Worse is Wont to Attack Better 16.56). While maintaining the God–master analogy to express the Jewish God's sovereignty (see also Josephus who, in Against Apion 2.35.247, points out that "some of the [Graeco-Roman] gods are slaves to human beings," providing examples from mythology), Philo also modifies and supplements traditional slavery metaphors to make them suitable to his own worldview and philosophy.

In rabbinic literature, theological matters tend to be expressed in parables, in which the narrative with images from daily life (*Bildebene*) serves as a metaphor for a higher truth (*Sachebene*). In later rabbinic slave parables, the "king" [*melekh*] is presented as a slave master (on king parables in general, see Ziegler 1903; Stern 1994: 19–21). The "king" is used as a metaphor for God or as his worldly alter ego, depending on his behavior toward his slaves. Several reasons can be adduced for the rabbinic preference for the "king" metaphor for God. In the first four centuries rabbis lived in a political context in which the Roman emperor was the highest authority, not only in Roman Italy but also in the provinces. When imagining God's hierarchical distance from and power over human beings, the emperor provided the closest worldly analogy. Second, the king metaphor provided a wider range of narrative options and meanings than the image of the civilian householder and slave owner. Besides slaves, the king could have other types of subordinates whom he treated differently or who could be compared with each other. Last but not least, the king would be even more distant from the slave than an ordinary master, being absent from his own landholdings and represented by servile managers and intermediaries. The king represented the transcendence and omnipotence of God better than the wealthy householder (see, for example, Luke's transformation of an ordinary house-holder into a royal contender in his version of the *peculium* parable in Luke 19:12).

The king's/God's spatial distance from his human "slave," which only he is in a position to narrow down, is expressed in a midrashic parable transmitted at the beginning of Leviticus Rabbah 1:7:

> To what can the matter be compared? To a king who commanded his slave and said to him: Build me a palace. On everything which he built, he wrote the name of the king. He built the walls and wrote on them the name of the king. He set up pillars and wrote on them the name of the king. He roofed it with beams and wrote on them the name of the king. After some time the king entered the palace. On everything which he saw he found his name written. He said: My slave has done me all this honor, and I am inside while he is outside. Call him that he may come inside!

In the midrashic context the parable is used to illustrate Moses' building of the tabernacle (related to Lev. 1:1 here; see also Ex. 25–31 and 35–40 and Num. 4:1–35). As an oral tradition transmitted independently from its current literary context the parable could relate to other buildings set up for the worship of God, such as the Jerusalem Temple and the late antique synagogue, which seems to have been perceived as a "holy place" in which worshipers felt close to God (on late antique synagogues as "holy places," see Schwartz 2001: 248; Zangenberg 2016: 168). Just as the king had his palace, built by his slaves, God had his special places on earth that were constructed by local Jews. Perceived as a "holy place" by means of its interior decoration, presence of Torah scrolls, and liturgical service, the synagogue was a place where the otherwise distant God could be considered near, enabling his worshipers to approach his domain.

God's Orders and Human Obeisance

The second commonality between the slave–master relationship and the Israelite and Jewish perception of God is the notion of the master/God issuing instructions to his slaves/Israelites and the latter's obligation to observe them, since nonobservance will result in punishment. This aspect is so prominent in the Hebrew Bible that it needs no further explication. The Israelite God revealed his commandments and legal rules to Moses at Sinai (Ex. 19–23), emphasizing that if the Israelites "listen to my voice and observe my covenant" (Ex. 19:5), they will stand in a special relationship to God. The Israelites allegedly replied that they "will do all" that God has commanded them (19:8). Whereas the oral commands liken the Israelite God to a human slave master, the idea of the covenant does not fit the *Bildfeld* (field of images) of slavery. After their purchase (purchase deeds are exchanged between the buyer and seller, not involving the slave him- or herself) slaves belong to the owner and can be put to work without the owner being obliged to anything in turn. By contrast, the biblical covenant between God and the Israelites is a mutual agreement like the work contract made between an employer and hired free laborers or alliance agreements between nations that involve obligations on both sides (McKenzie 2000; Elazar 2017).

In rabbinic parables this aspect of the slave–master relationship is expressed by the king giving orders to his slave/s. For example, Leviticus Rabbah 2:4 relates:

> R. Yudan in the name of R. Shmuel b. Nahman: A parable concerning a king who had an undergarment. And he commanded his slave and said to him: Fold it and shake it out and take care of it! He said to him: My master, king, of all the undergarments that you have you command me only concerning this one? He said to him: Because I wear it [close] to my body.
>
> Thus Moses said before the Holy One, blessed be He: Master of the Universe, from among the seventy distinct nations that you have in your world, you command me only concerning Israel? [As it is written,] 'Command the children of Israel' [Num. 28:2], 'Say to the children of Israel' [Ex. 33:5], 'Speak to the children of Israel' [Lev. 1:2].

In the midrashic application (*nimshal*) the "slave" is associated with Moses, whom God instructed in Lev. 1:2: "Speak to the children of Israel." In the midrashic context the parable is used to comment on this verse. The "undergarment" on which the king's orders focus is identified as Israel. All of God's commandments to Moses concern the Israelites only rather than any other nations. Moses appears as an intermediary or servile overseer here: He receives commands from God which Moses is supposed to direct to the Israelites, namely, to observe God's rules, as becomes clear from the biblical verses cited at the end of the text. In Leviticus Rabbah 2:4 two variants of the parable follow (see also the parallel in Pesiqta de Rav Kahana 2:7), which all express the same idea, namely, that among all nations only the Israelites have been chosen by God as worthy of receiving his commandments.

God's Punishment and Praise of His Human "Slaves"

Slave owners were known to severely punish slaves who disobeyed them, did something that their masters found offensive, or even talked back to them. The severity of punishment in the case of non-observance of God's commandments is expressed in another rabbinic parable in the same Midrash (Lev. R. 12:1):

> R. Pinhas [said] in the name of R. Levi on that which R. Yishmael [said]: [The matter may be compared] to a king who had appointed a trustworthy domestic. And [when] his agent stood at the door of a shop, he severed his head in silence and appointed another domestic in his place. And we only know why he killed the first from what the king commanded the second, saying to him: Do not enter the shop! We know that because of this he killed the first [domestic].
>
> Thus it is written here: 'And there came forth fire from before the Lord, and devoured them, and they died before the Lord' [Lev. 10:2]. We do not know why they [Nadab and Abihu, cf. Lev. 10:1] died.

It seems that the terms "domestic" and "agent" are used for one and the same person here. The first slave is severely punished by the king without knowledge of his transgression. No commandment to him is mentioned. The reason for his punishment becomes clear only from the king's order to the second slave. Obviously, the first domestic entered the shop against the king's wishes. In the midrashic context of Leviticus Rabbah the parable is meant to illustrate the Nadab and Abihu story: "And the sons of Aaron, Nadab and Abihu, took their censers, put fire in them, and laid upon it incense, and offered before the Lord a strange fire, which He had not commanded them" (Lev. 10:1), whereupon they were punished by fire that was issued by God (10:2). Nadab and Abihu did not transgress an explicit negative commandment but were punished severely for an action that displeased God. The biblical tradition and rabbinic parable suggest that God may even punish behaviors for which the Torah does not contain explicit prohibitions. Like human slave owners' harsh treatments of their slaves, for which no immediate reason may be evident, God can punish his human "slaves" for actions whose offensiveness may elude the practitioners.

Besides punishments, slave owners could praise and reward their slaves if they were satisfied with them. This aspect of slave–master relationship is also used theologically and given expression in rabbinic slave parables. For example, Leviticus Rabbah 1:15 transmits two parables that thematize a king's variant attitudes toward their slaves. The king of the first parable "was angry at his slave and ordered him to be confined in prison. When he commands his agent, he commands only from outside." By contrast, the second parable refers to the "tent of meeting," where God "is pleased with his children and domestics and his children and domestics are pleased with him. When he commands the agent, he commands only from inside, like one who places his son on his knees and like the hand of a human being on his son." In the second parable, the image of God as an uncompromising slave master changes into that of a loving father who caresses his child. A contrast is drawn between the master's anger and the slave's imprisonment on the one hand and the master's satisfaction with his slaves and his loving kindness toward them. The "insider" relationship is that of the household and family, represented by the "tent of meeting," whereas the "outsider" relationship is that of the disobedient slave whom his master has banned from his presence.

Slaves and Sons

Some slave parables compare and contrast the "slave's" and "son's" relationship to the king (Hezser 2005: 350–356, with examples). As already pointed out, both seem to represent options in God's relationship to humans: If they obey him, they are treated like children, but if they disobey, they are treated like slaves (Pes.R. 27 [28]). In the first case, voluntary practice is envisioned, whereas in the second case, force is involved. Rabbis were well aware of the stringencies and hardships involved in the slave–master relationship. While God can appear as strict as a slave master, the Divine can also be experienced differently by those who follow the rules of the Torah and rabbinic halakhah. Parables about God as a slave master versus a loving father were meant to encourage Torah observance. If this observance is not carried out properly, God has the option to force obeisance, just as a master forces a slave to fulfil his orders. That a "son" can easily become a "slave" is expressed in the following parable transmitted in Sifre Num. 115 (Hezser 2005: 352):

> To what may the matter be compared? To a king, the son of whose beloved was taken captive. But when he redeemed him, he did not redeem him as a free person but as a slave, so that if he issued a decree and he would not accept it, he would say to him: 'You are my slave' ... Likewise, when the Holy One, Blessed be He, redeemed the seed of Abraham His beloved, He did not redeem them as sons but as slaves. When he issues a decree and they do not accept [it], He can say to them: 'You are my slaves.'

The parable indicates why the slave–master relationship to God is still valid after the Exodus experience of liberation from slavery in Egypt. Israelites/Jews were redeemed by God, but they were redeemed as his "slaves," so that he can force them to follow his commandments and punish them, if they refrain from doing so voluntarily.

In ancient Christian texts the "son" and "slave" terminology is used differently and in self-distinction from Judaism. In 1 Corinthians Paul seems to identify circumcision (and, by extension, Torah observance) with being a "slave," whereas belief in Christ is seen as "freedom." Although he emphasizes that both circumcised (Jewish, cf. Collman 2023: 27–28) and uncircumcised (pagan) Christians are welcome and do not need to change their status (7:18–24), he nevertheless assumes that "freedom" is available through belief in Christ only and that those who were "slaves" (of the Torah?) should become "slaves of Christ": "For he who was called in the Lord [*kyrios*, identified with Christ here] being a slave is the Lord's free man. Likewise he who was called being free is Christ's slave" (7:22). Paul contrasts "slaves" and "sons" in Galatians 3:28–4:3 (Garnsey 1997: 105–108), in the famous passage about there being neither Jew nor Greek, neither slave nor free, neither male nor female in Christ (3:28). As Abraham's children Christians are declared "heirs" to the "estate" (3:29–4:1). For minor children, guardians and trustees are needed until they are sufficiently mature (4:2). Paul believes that he and his fellow Galatian Christians have left that stage and are no longer "slaves to the elemental spirits of the universe." As recognized children they now claim access to their patriarchal heritage: "So through God you are no longer a slave, but a son; and if a son then an heir" (4:7). Delaney (1998: 147) understands the text similarly: "Jews who merely followed the law and practices are enslaved, according to Paul; only belief in Jesus Christ would set them free."

The notion that Jews are "enslaved to the law," whereas only Christians are truly free is also expressed in Galatians 4:22–26:

> For it is written that Abraham had two sons, one by a slave woman and one by a free woman. But the son of the slave woman was born according to the flesh [*kata sarka*], the son of the free woman through promise [*di epaggelias*]. Now this is an allegory: these are two covenants. One is from Mount Sinai, bearing

children to slavery [*eis douleian*], which is Hagar. For this Hagar is Mount Sinai in Arabia, and answers to the Jerusalem that exists now, for she is enslaved [*douleuei*] with her children. But the Jerusalem that is above is free [*eleuthera*], which is the mother of us.

Paul declares Jews the offspring of Hagar here, identifying them with Ishmael, whereas Christians are seen as the children of Sarah, that is, they are identified with Isaac and Jacob (Delaney 1998: 147). Paul uses the biblical metaphor of the "slave," which Israelites and Jews used to express their relationship to God, against Jews here by claiming that Jews have a servile origin through their alleged descendance from a slave woman (Hagar), whereas Christians are elevated to the status of freeborn children as the "true" children of Abraham and Sarah. He seems to be aware of the Roman (and later rabbinic) legal rule that the status of children follows that of their mother if the mother is a slave, a regulation that is absent from the Hebrew Bible, where Hagar's children are legitimate heirs and sons of their father Abraham (Hezser 2005: 194–201). Paul delegitimizes the Sinai covenant, Jerusalem, and Jews in general here in order to claim the superiority of Christianity as the new covenant, Abraham's heirs, and spiritual Jerusalem (on this text see also Niehoff 2020).

The "slave"/"son" dichotomy also appears in later Christian texts, for example, in Clement of Alexandria (Exhortation to the Heathen 1.9), where God's "father" relationship to Christians as his "children" is emphasized: "for He desires us from slaves to become sons, while they scorn to become sons. Oh the prodigious folly of being ashamed of the Lord! He offers freedom, you flee into slavery." It seems that pagans who resist the Christian message are targeted here. Garnsey (1997: 108) has examined Lactantius' and Augustine's uses of the terminology. In Lactantius' writings, the "slave"/"son" terminology appears in the context of his polemics against polytheism (Divine Institutes) and in his presentation of an angry and merciful God (On Anger). Rather than associating the terms with different ethnic groups, as Paul (Jews as "slaves") and Clement of Alexandria (pagans as "slaves") did, Lactantius seems "to elide the distinction between son and slave" (Garnsey 1997: 108), emphasizing that God can be both "father" and "master," expressing mercy and anger, as is also evident in Roman law: "That master and father are one is established by civil law doctrine" (Lactantius, Divine Institutes 4.3.14–15, quoted in Garnsey 1997: 108). Both (minor) children and slaves were dependents of the householder and treated, to some extent, in similar fashion by him (Hezser 2005: 70–82). Lactantius merges the father/master (God) and the son/slave (Christians) as two aspects of one and the same human relationship to God (Divine Institutes 4.3.15–17). Augustine, on the other hand, reverts to the "slave"/ "son" distinction, which he associates with "fear" of the master and "love" between father and son (Garnsey 1997: 113). Yet the Christian martyr as a "good slave" can become a "son" in his relationship with God (Garnsey 1997: 113–114).

God's Ownership of Humans

The fourth commonality between the institution of slavery and ancient Jewish perceptions of God is the notion of ownership. Once slaves are in their master's possession, the master has full ownership over their bodies and can use them in accordance with his or her requirements and desires. This means that slaves are asked to carry out a variety of tasks in agriculture and in the household. Whereas the sources usually focus on the slave-free dichotomy, in reality the roles and statuses of slaves varied considerably from the simple farm worker to the highly educated secretary and business manager. For female (and also some beautiful young male) slaves ownership over their bodies included sexual exploitation. Although the master's ownership of his slave's mind may have been more difficult to achieve, preventing slaves from reaching their full intellectual potential and from carrying out their native religious practices may be considered spiritual coercion. As we have already seen, slaves working in Jewish households were customarily circumcised and immersed and slaves in Christian households were baptized, that is, they were subjected to physical rituals which had a higher, spiritual significance at least as far as the owners were concerned.

To what extent are these aspects of slavery reflected in the metaphorical realm? Already in the Hebrew Bible the universe and all that is in it, including humans, is said to have been created by God (Gen. 1–2). According to Job 41:11, "everything under heaven belongs to me"; Psalm 24:1 states: "The earth is the Lord's, and all it holds, the world and those that dwell in it"; and in Isa. 43:1 God introduces himself as "He who created you, Jacob; He who formed you, Israel . . . you are mine." God is imagined as the one who gives and takes life, that is, as someone who has power over a person's life and death. As Greene (2017) has pointed out in his chapter on "The Supreme Owner God," "[e]ven though people seldom talk about divine ownership, it is unavoidable to deal with this, because the idea that God really is the ultimate owner of the universe is a largely unanalyzed concept that haunts theology." According to Greene, "[i]t's a disturbing image because of what we know of human owners and how they often ruin and/or abuse their property" (Greene 2017). It is also disturbing because it may reduce humans to "objects" without agency, self-determination, and responsibility. In biblical theology, the notions of divine ownership, divine providence, and human free will are difficult to reconcile (Keuss 2010: 135; Krüger 2021: 24). If they are perceived in analogy to the institution of slavery, one may argue that slaves who are owned by their master are punished by him for their wrongdoing, that is, they are held responsible for their actions despite being considered non-persons and property from the legal point of view. As part of creation but appointed as "rulers" over other creatures (Gen. 1:26), humans may have been perceived as caretakers within the ancient servile hierarchy.

The Privilege of Being God's "Slave"

In rabbinic texts, the notion of God's ownership of Jews is linked to the covenantal relationship that involves Torah observance and the chosenness of the Israelites/Jews as God's people. As long as Jews observe their God's/master's commandments, they belong to him; once they stop doing so, they are considered to have other masters. Lev. 20:26 states: "You are to be holy to me because I, the Lord, am holy, and I have set you apart from the nations to be my own." In Sifra, the tannaitic Midrash on Leviticus, this verse is explained as follows: "If you are separate from the people [i.e. other nations], you are mine; if not, you are Nevuchadnezzar's and his fellows'." According to the rabbinic interpretation, Jews' actions decide whether or not they belong to God. Belonging to God is considered the privilege of those who observe the Torah and thereby accept "enslavement" to God. Not being God's "slave" does not mean freedom, however, but rather enslavement to human political leaders who, at the time of the composition of Sifra, would have been Roman. The midrash ends by stressing that a person belonging to God "separates from sin and accepts upon himself the yoke of the kingdom of heaven" (Sifra Kedoshim 9:12). Similarly, the Mekhilta de R. Yishmael specifies: "R. Yishmael says: When you are holy, you are mine" (22:30). Like slave owners, who choose the slaves they decide to purchase and sell those they are dissatisfied with, God decides whom he keeps as his slave. The texts emphasize the necessity of the "slaves'" diligent "work" for their divine master, that is, the observance of the Torah and rabbinic rules.

Whereas Paul generally prefers the term "sons" for Christians, he also uses the term "slave" for himself and Apollo in the sense of being chosen by God to be a religious leader. Already at the beginning of Romans, Paul introduces himself as a "slave of Jesus Christ, called to be an apostle, separated for the gospel of God" (1:1). There is a striking terminological similarity between this text and Sifra Kedoshim 9:11–12: Just as Jews/rabbis are separated (*perush*) from others to observe the Torah, Paul is set apart (*aporismenos*) to be God's/Christ's apostle. Slaves who are elevated by their master and appointed to special roles constitute the real-life background of this rhetoric. Doering (2012: 455) has suggested that Paul's use of the title "slave of Jesus Christ" "merges the authorisation of high-ranking Christ-believing leaders ... with the designation of extraordinary figures in the OT and early Judaism, like Moses, David, and the patriarchs (N.B. Jacob), or the prophets, that is, 'slave of God' ... The *intitulatio* thus styles the addressor as a high-ranking Christ-believing functionary in the tradition of exemplary biblical figures." The self-identification as a specially chosen "slave of God" may also have involved competition with Pharisees (and later rabbis), who associated such a relationship with Torah observance. A term that, in real life, denotes individuals at the very bottom of or even outside of the social hierarchy is used as a title of privilege by religious functionaries (Paul and other apostles, rabbis) to express their special relationship to God.

In 1 Corinthians 4:1–2, Paul presents himself and Apollo as "stewards" or managers of his household (*oikonomoi*): "So let a man think of us as Christ's servants (*hyperetas*), and stewards (*oikonomous*) of God's mysteries. Here, moreover, it is required of stewards, that they be found faithful (*pistos*)." Clearly, the language of slavery is used here. The term *hyperetes* denoted the household slave (Agosto 2005: 177). Slave *oikonomoi* were set as overseers and managers over other slaves (see also Martin 1990: 14–16). They had to be particularly skilled and trustworthy to be allocated that role. Paul's use of the terms *oikonomos* and *pistos* are reminiscent of the "faithful steward (*pistos oikonomos*), whom his master shall set over his household" during his absence (Luke 12:42). Paul identified himself with the "faithful steward" who manages the early Christian communities until his "master's" return. According to Lim (2017: 130), Paul uses the slavery metaphors in a context in which his leadership role was questioned to explain "his role, rights, and responsibilities as an apostle," who functioned as an intermediary between the Divine and ordinary Christians.

The Maidservant Mary as the Victim of Divine Rape

Whereas Paul identifies himself as the "household manager" of the Divine, in the gospel of Luke, Mary, the mother of Jesus, introduces herself as "the maidservant of the Lord [*doulē kyriou*]" (1:38), a term that is never associated with her in the other gospels. Female slaves had to endure sexual exploitation from their masters. Is the slavery imagery, perhaps, carried too far here to suggest that Mary was sexually (ab)used by her "master" (God/the Holy Spirit) and gave birth to his child? Luke would have been well aware of the connotations of the "female slave" image and used the term to express Mary's humility and obedience to serve her "master" with her entire body. In Mary's prayer (1:48) the term is paired with "lowliness" and contrasted with God's might and strength (1:49, 51). As a lowly woman, Mary would have been unable to resist the advances of her powerful "master." Ancient audiences, especially if they were female, may have understood Mary's impregnation as a kind of "holy rape," a notion that is also known from Graeco-Roman mythology, where male gods enter into sexual relations with female human beings. In her study of *parthenoi* ("virgins"; the term is associated with Mary in Matth. 1:22–3, where the prophecy of Isa. 7:14 is quoted) and rape in Greek myth, Deacy (1997: 43) investigates the issue of "sexual vulnerability." The *parthenoi* "are typically represented as incapable of resisting sex through their own initiative and as subject to some degree of sexual coercion" (Deacy 1997: 43).

Feminist scholars have criticized Mary's subordination and "rape" in Christian literature and iconography: "Like all rape victims in male myth she submits joyously to this unspeakable degradation" (Mary Daly 1984: 74, quoted in Boss 2000: 9; see also Waller 2015: 60 for further feminist reactions to this problematic idea). Waller has shown that the church fathers and church leaders usually reacted to Luke's representation of "a sado-masochistic relationship of compulsion, subordination, and fear" with "responses that today may read like defenses of rape – either that it is a privilege to be overwhelmed by a divine being or that the victim's response is, despite appearances to the contrary, really freely given" (Waller 2015: 61). The notion that a young woman presented as a "female slave" of a divine master was raped by the Holy Spirit, which constitutes the basis of the Christian creed, remains highly problematic from both a feminist and an abolitionist perspective.

If the slavery metaphors were carried further, as the son of a an (albeit metaphorical) "female slave" (Luke 1:38, 48) Jesus would have had "slave" status himself (for Roman and rabbinic law on "illegitimate unions" between female slaves and free men, see Hezser 2005: 194–201). Even if Mary was imagined as a free married woman, a child conceived outside of marriage would be considered a *mamzer* (bastard) according to Jewish law. Jesus' birth story is often maligned in rabbinic sources (on her representation in rabbinic literature, see Visotzky 1990 and Himmelfarb 2020) at a time when Byzantine church fathers, especially representatives of the Eastern Church, glorified her as the Theothokos ("the one who gave birth to God"). In the Byzantine liturgical tradition, the "Song of Mary" or "Ode of the Theotokos" was the *Magnificat*, based on Luke 1:46–55, that is, Mary's self-identification as a *doulē* became a central aspect of Catholic religiosity. According to Wilson (2015: 92), the song associated Mary with biblical "slaves" of God and expressed a religious status reversal from humility to exaltation and glory.

Jesus and Jewish Charismatics as "Sons" of God

Whereas Luke refers to slaves frequently and transmits several slave parables, he never calls Jesus the "slave" of God. By contrast, Matthew (12:18) associates Jesus with the prophecy of Deutero-Isaiah 42:1, where the term *pais mou*, "my servant," is used as a translation of the Hebrew *avdi*, "my slave." Luke's reluctance to use the slave metaphor for Jesus may partly be due to the Hellenistic context in which he wrote. Another, perhaps related, reason was his Christology that distinguished Jesus from both biblical leadership figures and contemporary Christian leaders of his own church. Therefore, the terms most often applied to Jesus in Luke are *epistatēs*, "overseer," "superintendent" (used by the disciples, for example 8:24), and *kyrios*, "lord" (used by ordinary people, for example, 6:46; 7:6,13), a term that Luke also uses for God (e.g., 2:9,15).

The term most frequently used for Jesus in all three synoptic gospels is "son of God" (see already Mark 1:1). In the scene where John baptizes Jesus, a heavenly voice is quoted saying: "You are my beloved son, with whom I am pleased" (1:11). While the use of the "son" metaphor has a christological meaning here, it also appears in rabbinic texts to express a wise man's intimate and familiar relationship to God. In the mishnaic story about Honi the rainmaker (m. Taan. 3:8), Honi prays to God: "Master of the World, your children have turned to me, because I am like a son of the household [*ben bayyit*] before you." At the end of the narrative, Shimon b. Shetach acknowledges Honi's special relationship to God: "You ask petulantly before the Omnipresent and he fulfils your wish, like a son who asks his father petulantly and he fulfils his wish. And upon you Scripture says: 'May your father and mother be glad and may she who gave birth to you rejoice!' (Proverbs 23:25)." Green considers the acknowledgment of Honi's exceptional relationship to God a first step toward the rabbinization of this charismatic figure (Green 1979: 638). The title "Rabbi" is attributed to him in the Babylonian Talmud only (b. Taanit 23a), where another charismatic, Hanina b. Dosa, is also called "son" by a heavenly voice (b. Taanit 24b; on Hanina as a wonder-worker, see Bokser 1985). The rabbinic association of the "son" metaphor with individual charismatic figures suggests that it was not a common term that rabbis used for themselves. It presumed a closeness and familiarity with the Divine that was considered inappropriate in view of God's otherness and transcendence. Rabbis may have been aware of the Christian use of the title "son of God" for Jesus. This may have been an additional reason why they hesitated to use it more often themselves.

Conclusions

Slavery metaphors are widely used in the foundational texts of Judaism, Christianity, and Islam, and are based on the tradents' and editors' familiarity with slaves, slave owners, and slave practices in the ancient and late antique contexts they lived in. Slave terminology is part of the anthropomorphic speech about God which projects human power relationships onto the divine sphere. The result is a theology that replicates central aspects of the slave–master relationship such as status hierarchy, ownership, and the duty to carry out all of the master's instructions or suffer severe punishment. An institution that is nowadays considered deeply problematic and fraud with abuse, discrimination, and inequality has not only informed but also moulded monotheistic theology. The challenge therefore is how to deal with this phenomenon and approach the ancient texts from an anti-slavery perspective. At a time when real-life slavery has been abolished officially – notwithstanding the continuity of various forms of forced labor – should metaphorical enslavement persist and determine monotheistic theology and practice? Just as feminism questioned the idea of a male God and Holocaust theologians challenged the biblical notions of God's justice and mercy, the perception of God as a slave master and humans as his slaves requires a revision because it is based on the ancient acceptance of an institution that is nowadays considered socially and morally wrong.

The metaphor of slavery is not only central to biblical monotheism and post-biblical monotheistic religions. In politics, philosophy, and psychoanalysis, slavery metaphors have determined western culture from antiquity onward. DuBois (2003: 139) has shown that "[t]he historians and other writers of the classical period used the language of slavery . . . as an almost technical political language, deploying it as a metaphor to invoke possibilities of domination and submission." As a political metaphor, slavery is linked to the rhetoric of war and imperialism. Another aspect is the philosophical use of slavery metaphors from Plato (e.g., Laws 726a) onward to express humans' alleged domination by their emotions and desires. The rhetoric is part of the call for self-discipline that is of central significance in Stoic philosophy (e.g., Epictetus, Enchiridion 14; Seneca, Letters 47.20; Cicero, Sulla 8) and religious asceticism. It resurfaces in Freudian psychoanalytical theory, where the Superego controls the Id to achieve the rational state of mind associated with the Ego. In *Moses and Monotheism*, Freud (1939: 149) draws a direct link between the Superego as the "master" and the Ego's enslavement to it: "It keeps the Ego in lasting dependence and exercises a steady pressure. The Ego is concerned, just as it was in childhood, to retain the love of its master." In his critique of Freudian theory, Elliot (1999: 38) writes: "Through situating authority in direct relation to the constitution of the superego, Freud's tripartite model of the psyche provides a particularly rich account of the ways in which social relations of domination and exploitation are reproduced and sustained."

The two major shortcomings of slavery metaphors are their inability to account for human autonomy and their attribution of normativity to an institution that must be rejected on moral grounds. How, then, can a critique of slavery practices lead to a critique of metaphorical enslavement, as far as Jewish monotheism is concerned? The ancient sources may point the way toward changes and adjustments. The Hebrew Bible supplements slavery metaphors with other images taken from the *Bildfeld* of the family. God was not only seen as a slave master but also as the loving father (Perdue 1997: 225–234; Carroll 2003: 116–121) and mother (Claassens 2012: 41–63) of the Israelites, who supported them and expressed his or her affection. The notion that Israelites/ Jews were the "children" of God continued in postbiblical and rabbinic writings and expressed more benign and emotional aspects of the relationship between humans and God. Claassens also points to the images of God as mourner and midwife in biblical texts (Claassens 2012: 18–40 and 64–79). Another metaphorical field is friendship, applied in Philo's reference to the wise as "friends" of God. These and other metaphors that are less prominent than the master/slave imagery may be discovered and reinterpreted.

The ancient tradents and editors were already aware of the phenomenon that none of the metaphors they used could sufficiently express their experiences with the Divine. Therefore, they combined images from different areas of life – slavery, family, law courts – although they might be contradictory, without combining them into a theological system. Rather, the metaphors are used side by side without any attempt at explaining and harmonizing them. Furthermore, rabbis pointed to differences between the behaviors of human kings and slave owners and God. Some of the king parables are followed by the disclaimer that God "is not like" the king "of flesh and blood." In such instances the parable functions as a counter-metaphor for rabbis' perception of God, revealing a negative theology rather than an attempt to fixate God in anthropomorphic terms. While using traditional metaphors such as those taken from the *Bildfeld* of slavery, rabbis were aware of and emphasized God's otherness, which could not be captured in words and images devised by humans.

All ancient literary representations of God were conceived from an androcentric perspective that paid little attention to women's experiences, especially those of female slaves. From the perspective of ancient Jewish women, for whom enslavement would have evoked images of sexual abuse, the slave/ master metaphor was doubly problematic. The image of the dominating master who requires total subordination from his slave had different meanings for men and women, not least because men also applied it to the husband–wife relationship. As Bjelland Kartzov (2018) has already emphasized, the metaphorical "freedom" from slavery, celebrated in the Passover ritual and in Paul's insistence that there is "neither slave nor free," would have been perceived differently by married women who were "owned" by and expected to "serve" their husband (*ba'al*).

Ultimately, slavery metaphors may express the human experience that freedom is always limited, that total freedom can never be achieved. Even if freedom of decision-making and action are guaranteed, one is always at least to some extent bound to the social, economic, political, geographical, and ecological circumstances one lives in. In Jewish monotheism, the dialectic between freedom and bondage are expressed in the narrative of the Exodus, followed by the revelation of the Torah at Sinai. Divine redemption from slavery is followed by the divine institution of laws that are meant to perpetually guide one's actions: "For Jewish thought, human freedom and divine command are a paradoxical, subtle unity. The command is a command only when freely received and the freedom a freedom only when divinely given" (Morgan 1992: 76).

References

Agosto, E. (2005). *Servant Leadership: Jesus and Paul*. St. Louis, MO: Chalice Press.

Ali, K. (2010). *Marriage and Slavery in Early Islam*. Cambridge, MA: Harvard University Press.

Aminof, I. (2015). *Esau My Brother: Father of Edom and Rome*. Jerusalem: Rubin Mass.

Ariel, D. S. (2006). *Kabbalah: The Mystic Quest in Judaism*. Lanham, MD: Rowman & Littlefield.

Bakhos, C. (2006). *Ishmael on the Border: Rabbinic Portrayals of the First Arab*. Albany, NY: State University of New York Press.

Bakhos, C. (2007). Figuring (Out) Esau: The Rabbis and Their Others. *Journal of Jewish Studies* 58, 250–262.

B. E. J. (1932). Review of: E. McKenna Friend, Moses Mielziner, 1828–1903: A Biography with a Bibliography of His Writings and a Reprint of His "Slavery Amongst the Ancient Hebrews." *Journal of American History* 19(1), 152.

Bjelland Kartzow, M. (2018). *The Slave Metaphor and Gendered Enslavement in Early Christian Discourse: Double Trouble Embodied*. Abingdon: Routledge.

Bokser, B. M. (1984). *The Origins of the Seder: The Passover Rite and Early Rabbinic Judaism*. Berkeley, CA: University of California Press.

Bokser, B. M. (1985). Wonder-Working and the Rabbinic Tradition: The Case of Hanina ben Dosa. *Journal for the Study of Judaism* 16, 42–92.

Boss, S. J. (2000). *Empress and Handmaid: On Nature and Gender in the Cult of the Virgin Mary*. London: Cassell.

Bradley, K. (1994). *Slavery and Society at Rome*. Cambridge: Cambridge University Press.

Bradley, K. (2000). Animalizing the Slave: The Truth of Fiction. *Journal of Roman Studies* 90, 110–125.

Bradley, K. & Cartledge, P., eds. (2011). *The Cambridge World History of Slavery, Vol. 1: The Ancient Mediterranean World*. Cambridge: Cambridge University Press.

Bridge, E. J. (2010). *The Use of Slave Terms in Deference and in Relation to God in the Hebrew Bible*. Unpublished PhD thesis, Macquarie University, Sydney.

Bridge, E. J. (2013). The Metaphorical Use of Slave Terms in the Hebrew Bible. *Bulletin for Biblical Research* 23, 13–28.

Bridge, E. J. (2014). The "Slave" Is the "Master": Jacob's Servile Language to Esau in Genesis 33.1–17. *Journal for the Study of the Old Testament* 38, 263–278.

Buckland, W. W. (1970, reprint of 1908). *The Roman Law of Slavery: The Condition of the Slave in Private Law from Augustus to Justinian*. Cambridge: Cambridge University Press.

Byron, J. (2003). *Slavery Metaphors in Early Judaism and Pauline Christianity: A Traditio-historical and Exegetical Examination*. Tübingen: Mohr Siebeck.

Carroll, M. D. (2003). Family in the Prophetic Literature. In: R. S. Hess & M. D. Carroll (eds.), *Family in the Bible: Exploring Customs, Culture, and Context*. Grand Rapids, MI: Baker Academic, pp. 100–123.

Chen, K. S. (2019). *The Messianic Vision of the Exodus*. Downers Grove, IL: Intervarsity Press.

Chirichigno, G. C. (1993). *Debt-Slavery in Israel and the Ancient Near East*. Sheffield: JSOT Press.

Claassens, L. J. M. (2012). *Mourner, Mother, Midwife: Reimagining God's Delivering Presence in the Old Testament*. Louisville, KY: Westminster John Knox Press.

Cohen, S. J. D. (2005). *Why Aren't Jewish Women Circumcised? Gender and Covenant in Judaism*. Berkeley: University of California Press.

Colish, M. L. (1985). *The Stoic Tradition from Antiquity to the Early Middle Ages, Vol. 1: Stoicism in Classical Latin Literature*. Leiden: Brill.

Collman, R. D. (2023). *The Apostle to the Foreskin: Circumcision in the Letters of Paul*. Berlin: Walter de Gruyter.

Cook, D. (1984). Joseph and Aseneth. In: H. F. D. Sparks (ed.), *The Apocryphal Old Testament*. Oxford: Oxford University Press, 465–504. www.markgoo-dacre.org/aseneth/translat.htm

Daly, M. (1984). *Pure Lust: Elemental Feminist Philosophy*. Boston, MA: Women's Press.

Dan, J. (1986). Introduction. In: J. Dan (ed.), *The Early Kabbalah*. New York: Paulist Press, 43–44.

Deacy, S. (1997). The Vulnerability of Athena: Parthenoi and Rape in Greek Myth. In: S. Deacy & K. F. Pierce (eds.), *Rape in Antiquity: Sexual Violence in the Greek and Roman Worlds*. London: Duckworth, pp. 43–64.

Delaney, C. (1998). *Abraham on Trial: The Social Legacy of Biblical Myth*. Princeton, NJ: Princeton University Press.

Devries, L. (1997). Baal. In W. E. Mills (ed.), *Mercer Dictionary of the Bible.* 5th ptg. Macon, GA: Mercer University Press, pp. 79–80.

Di Segni, L. (1988). The Inscriptions of Tiberias (Hebrew). *Idan* 11, 70–95.

Dobbs, D. (1994). Natural Right and the Problem of Aristotles' Defense of Natural Slavery. *Journal of Politics* 56, 69–94.

Doering, L. (2012). *Ancient Jewish Letters and the Beginnings of Christian Epistolography.* Tübingen: Mohr Siebeck.

Drescher, S. (2010). Jews and New Christians in the Atlantic Slave Trade. In: J. D. Sarna & A. Mendelsohn (eds.), *Jews and the Civil War: A Reader.* New York: New York University Press, pp. 51–86.

DuBois, P. (2003). *Slaves and Other Objects.* Chicago, IL: University of Chicago Press.

Elazar, D. J. (2017). *Covenant and Polity in Biblical Israel: Biblical Foundations & Jewish Expressions.* London: Routledge.

Elliot, A. (1999). *Social Theory and Psychoanalysis in Transition: Self and Society from Freud to Kristeva.* London: Routledge.

El-Sharif, A. (2012). Metaphors We Believe By: Islamic Doctrine as Evoked by the Prophet Muhammad's Metaphors. *Critical Discourse Studies* 9, 231–245.

Faber, E. (1998). *Jews, Slaves, and the Slave Trade: Setting the Record Straight.* New York: New York University Press.

Fagenblat, M., ed. (2017). *Negative Theology and Jewish Modernity.* Bloomington, IN: Indiana University Press.

Farbstein, D. (1896). *Das Recht der freien und unfreien Arbeiter nach jüdisch-talmudischem Recht verglichen mit dem antiken, speciell mit dem römischen Recht.* Frankfurt: Kauffmann.

Ferguson, E. (2003). *Backgrounds of Early Christianity.* 3rd ed. Grand Rapids, MI: William B. Eerdmans.

Forsdyke, S. (2021). *Slaves and Slavery in Ancient Greece.* Cambridge: Cambridge University Press.

Fraade, S. D. (1983). Sifre Deuteronomy 26 (ad Deut. 3:23): How Conscious the Composition? *Hebrew Union College Annual* 54, 245–301.

Frede, M. (1978). Principles of Stoic Grammar. In: J. M. Rist (ed.), *The Stoics.* Berkeley, CA: University of California Press, pp. 27–76.

Freud, S. (1939). *Moses and Monotheism.* London: Hogarth Press.

Friedman, S. S. (1998). *Jews and the American Slave Trade.* Piscataway, NJ: Transaction.

Garlitz, D. (2015). Judaism. In: L. Tendrich Frank (ed.), *The World of the Civil War: A Daily Life Encyclopedia.* Santa Barbara, CA: Greenwood, pp. 572–574.

Garnsey, P. (1994). Philo Judaeus and Slave Theory. *Scripta Classica Israelica* 13, 30–45.

Garnsey, P. (1996). *Ideas of Slavery from Aristotle to Augustine*. Cambridge: Cambridge University Press.

Garnsey, P. (1997). Sons, Slaves – and Christians. In: B. Rawson & P. Weaver (eds.), *The Roman Family in Italy: Status, Sentiment, Space*. Oxford: Oxford University Press, pp. 101–121.

Geary, D. & Hodkinson, S. (2012). Introduction: Slaves and Religions: Historiographies, Ancient and Modern. In: D. Geary & S. Hodkinson (eds.), *Slaves and Religions in Graeco-Roman Antiquity and Modern Brazil*. Newcastle upon Tyne: Cambridge Scholars.

Gerbner, K. (2018). *Christian Slavery: Conversion and Race in the Protestant Atlantic World*. Philadelphia, PA: University of Pennsylvania Press.

Giles, K. (1994). The Biblical Argument for Slavery: Can the Bible Mislead? A Case Study in Hermeneutics. *Evangelical Quarterly* 661, 3–17.

Giller, P. (2001). *Reading the Zohar: The Sacred Text of the Kabbalah*. Oxford: Oxford University Press.

Glancy, J. A. (2002). *Slavery in Early Christianity*. Oxford: Oxford University Press.

Glancy, J. A. (2011). *Slavery as Moral Problem: In the Early Church and Today*. Minneapolis, MN: Fortress Press.

Goldenberg, D. M. (2003). *The Curse of Ham: Race and Slavery in Early Judaism, Christianity, and Islam*. Princeton, NJ: Princeton University Press.

Goldman, E. (1992). Introduction. In: Y. Leibowitz, *Judaism, Human Values, and the Jewish State*, E. Goldman (ed.). Cambridge, MA: Harvard University Press, pp. vii-xxxiv.

Green, W. S. (1979). Palestinian Holy Men: Charismatic Leadership and Rabbinic Tradition. *Aufstieg und Niedergang der Römischen Welt II* 19.2, 619–647.

Greene, P. J. (2017). *The End of Divine Truthiness: Love, Power, and God: Powerful Buddhist-Christian-Taoist Love*. Eugene, OR: Wipf & Stock.

Grünfeld, R. (1886). *Die Stellung der Sclaven bei den Juden nach biblischen und talmudischen Quellen*, part 1. Doctoral thesis, University of Jena.

Hacohen, M. H. (2019). *Jacob & Esau: Jewish European History between Nation and Empire*. Cambridge: Cambridge University Press.

Hamel, G. H. (1990). *Poverty and Charity in Roman Palestine, First Three Centuries C.E.* Berkeley, CA: University of California Press.

Hamel, G. H. (2010). Poverty and Charity. In: C. Hezser (ed.), *The Oxford Handbook of Jewish Daily Life in Roman Palesti*ne. Oxford: Oxford University Press, pp. 308–324.

Harper, K. (2011). *Slavery in the Late Roman World, AD 275–425.* Cambridge: Cambridge University Press.

Harris, J. H. (1999). *Slave of Christ: A New Testament Metaphor for Total Devotion to Christ.* Downer's Grove, IL: InterVarsity Press.

Harris, W. V. (2001). *Restraining Rage: The Ideology of Anger Control in Classical Antiquity.* Cambridge, MA: Harvard University Press.

Haynes, S. R. (2002). *Noah's Curse: The Biblical Justification of American Slavery.* Oxford: Oxford University Press.

Heschel, A. J. (1951). *Man Is Not Alone: A Philosophy of Religion.* New York: Farrar, Straus & Giroux.

Heschel, A. J. (1959). *Between God and Man.* New York: Free Press.

Hezser, C. (1997). *The Social Structure of the Rabbinic Movement in Roman Palestine.* Tübingen: Mohr Siebeck.

Hezser, C. (2003). Slaves and Slavery in Rabbinic and Roman Law. In: C. Hezser (ed.), *Rabbinic Law in Its Roman and Near Eastern Context.* Tübingen: Mohr Siebeck, pp. 133–176.

Hezser, C. (2005). *Jewish Slavery in Antiquity.* Oxford: Oxford University Press.

Hezser, C. (2013). Part Whore, Part Wife: Slave Women in the Palestinian Rabbinic Tradition. In: U. E. Eisen, C. Gerber, & A. Standhartinger (eds.), *Doing Gender – Doing Religion. Fallstudien zur Intersektionalitaet im fruehen Judentum, Christentum und Islam.* Tübingen: Mohr Siebeck, pp. 303–323.

Hezser, C. (2016). Greek and Roman Slaving in Comparative Ancient Perspective: The Level of Integration. In: S. Hodkinson, M. Kleijwegt, and K. Vlassopoulos (eds.), *The Oxford Handbook of Greek and Roman Slaveries.* Oxford: Oxford University Press (online publication). https://academic.oup.com/edited-volume/40302

Hezser, C. (2018). *Bild und Kontext. Jüdische und christliche Ikonographie der Spätantike.* Tübingen: Mohr Siebeck.

Hezser, C. (2019). Women, Children, and Slaves in Rabbinic Law. In: P. Barmash (ed.), *The Oxford Handbook of Biblical Law.* Oxford: Oxford University Press, pp. 489–503.

Hezser, C. (2022). What Was Jewish about Jewish Slavery in Late Antiquity? In: C. L. de Wet, M. Kahlos & V. Vuolanto (eds.), *Slavery in the Late Antique World, 150–700 CE.* Cambridge: Cambridge University Press, pp. 129–148.

Hezser, C. (2023). New Testament and Rabbinic Slave Parables at the Intersection between Fiction and Reality. In: A. Merz, E. Ottenheijm, & N. Spoelstra (eds.), *The Power of Parables: Essays on the Comparative Study of Jewish and Christian Parables.* Leiden: Brill, pp. 367–388.

Hezser, C. (forthcoming). Passover, Liberation from Foreign Domination, and Roman-Byzantine Imperialism: The Exodus Tradition in Late Antique Judaism. In: F. López-Sánchez & M. Bueno-Sánchez (eds.), *The New Children of Israel: Newcomers in Movement from Constantine to Muhammad.*

Himmelfarb, M. (2020). The Virgin Mary and Ancient Jewish Literature. In: F. E. Consolino & J. Herrin (eds.), *The Early Middle Ages.* Atlanta, GA: SBL Press, pp. 103–120.

Hunt, P. (2018). *Ancient Greek and Roman Slavery.* Hoboken, NJ: Wiley Blackwell.

Ilan, T. (1995). *Jewish Women in Greco-Roman Palestine: An Inquiry into Image and Status.* Tübingen: Mohr Siebeck.

Isaac, B. (2004). *The Invention of Racism in Classical Antiquity.* Princeton, NJ: Princeton University Press.

Jensen, R. M. (forthcoming). *Understanding Early Christian Art.* 2nd ed. Abingdon: Routledge.

Joshel, S. R. (2010). *Slavery in the Roman World.* Cambridge: Cambridge University Press.

Kahlos, M. (2022). Late Roman Ideas of Ethnicity and Enslavement. In: C. L. de Wet, M. Kahlos & V. Vuolanto (eds.), *Slavery in the Late Antique World, 150–700 CE.* Cambridge: Cambridge University Press, pp. 87–104.

Kamen, D. (2023). *Greek Slavery.* Berlin: Walter de Gruyter.

Kasher, A. (1988). *Jews, Idumaeans, and Ancient Arabs: Relations of the Jews in Eretz-Israel.* Tübingen: Mohr Siebeck.

Keuss, J. F. (2010). *Freedom of the Self: Kenosis, Cultural Identity, and Mission at the Crossroads.* Eugene, OR: Wipf & Stock.

König, A. (1873/4). *Die Bibel und die Sklaverei.* Reisse: F. Bär.

Krauss, S. (1911, reprinted in1966). *Talmudische Archäologie*, Vol. 2. Leipzig, reprinted Hildesheim.

Krüger, P. P. (2021). Life in the Pentateuch (1): Genesis 1–11: Life Created and Sustained. In: A. J. Coetsee & F. P. Viljoen (eds.), *Biblical Theology of Life in the Old Testament.* Cape Town: AOSIS, pp. 11–34.

Kyrtatas, D. J. (1987). *The Social Structure of the Early Christian Communities.* New York: Verso.

Labowitz, G. (2009). *Marriage and Metaphor: Constructions of Gender in Rabbinic Literature.* Lanham, MD: Lexington Books.

Laitman, M. (2007). *The Zohar: Annotations to the Ashlag Commentary.* Toronto: Kabbalah.

Langer, G. (2010). Brother Esau? Esau in Rabbinic Midrash. In: A. Laato & P. Lindqvist (eds.), *Encounters of the Children of Abraham from Ancient to Modern Times.* Leiden: Brill, pp. 75-94.

Lewis, D. M. (2018). *Greek Slave Systems in Their Eastern Mediterranean Context, c.800–146 BC.* Oxford: Oxford University Press.

Lim, K. Y. (2017). *Metaphors and Social Identity Formation in Paul's Letters to the Corinthians.* Eugene, OR: Pickwick.

Lindemann, A. S. (1997). *Esau's Tears: Modern Anti-Semitism and the Rise of the Jews.* Cambridge: Cambridge University Press.

Lockyer, H. (1975). *All the Divine Names and Titles in the Bible.* Grand Rapids, MI: Zondervan.

Lowance, M. I. Jr., ed. (2003). *A House Divided: The Antebellum Slavery Debates in America, 1776–1865.* Princeton, NJ: Princeton University Press.

Martin, D. B. (1990). *Slavery as Salvation: The Metaphor of Slavery in Pauline Christianity.* New Haven, CT: Yale University Press.

McCraken Flesher, P. V. (1988). *Oxen, Women, or Citizens? Slaves in the System of the Mishnah.* Atlanta, GA: Brown Judaic Studies.

McKenzie, S. L. (2000). *Covenant.* St. Louis, MO: Chalice Press.

Meeks, W. A. (1983, 2nd ed. 2003). *The First Urban Christians: The Social World of the Apostle Paul.* New Haven, CT: Yale University Press.

Mendelsohn, I. (1978). *Slavery in the Ancient Near East: A Comparative Study of Slavery in Babylonia, Assyria, Syria, and Palestine from Middle of the Third Millennium to the End of the First Millennium.* Westport, CT: Greenwood Press.

Meyer, M. A. (1997). *Response to Modernity: A History of the Reform Movement in Judaism.* Detroit, MI: Wayne State University Press.

Mielziner, M. (1859). *Die Verhältnisse der Sklaven bei den alten Hebräern, nach biblischen und talmudischen Quellen dargestellt: Ein Beitrag zur hebräisch-jüdischen Alterthumskunde.* Copenhagen: P. G. Philipsen.

Mielziner, M. (1931). The Institution of Slavery among the Ancient Hebrews According to the Bible and Talmud (reprint). In: E. McKenna Friend Mielziner (ed.), *Moses Mielziner, 1828–1903: A Biography with a Bibliography of His Writings, with a Reprint of His "Slavery among the Ancient Hebrew."* New York: The Author. Originally published in Cincinnati, OH: The Bloch Printing Company, 1894, https://archive.org/details/mielzinerm1894isaah (no page numbers).

Miles, M. R. (1993). Santa Maria Maggiore's Fifth-Century Mosaics: Triumphal Christianity and the Jews. *Harvard Theological Review* 86, 155–176.

Miller, K. D. (2012). *Martin Luther King's Biblical Epic: His Final, Great Speech.* Jackson, MS: University Press of Mississippi.

Morgan, M. L. (1992). *Dilemmas in Modern Jewish Thought: The Dialectics of Revelation and History.* Bloomington, IN: Indiana University Press.

Murphy, C. (2002). *Wealth in the Dead Sea Scrolls and in the Qumran Community*. Leiden, MA: Brill.

Niehoff, M. R. (2018). *Philo of Alexandria: An Intellectual Biography*. New Haven, CT: Yale University Press.

Niehoff, M. R. (2020). Abraham in the Greek East: Faith, Circumcision, and Covenant in Philo's Allegorical Commentary and Paul's Letter to the Galatians. *The Studia Philonica Annual* 32, 227–248.

Noll, M. A. (2006). *The Civil War as a Theological Crisis*. Chapel Hill, NC: University of North Carolina Press.

Noy, D. (1993). *Jewish Inscriptions from Western Europe, Vol. 1: Italy (excluding the City of Rome), Spain and Gaul*. Cambridge: Cambridge University Press.

Oehler, G. F. (1891). *Theologie des Alten Testaments*. Stuttgart: J. F. Steinkopf.

Orlov, A. A. (2005). *The Enoch-Metatron Tradition*. Tübingen: Mohr Siebeck.

Owens, W. M. (2022). *The Representation of Slavery in the Greek Novel: Resistance and Appropriation*. London: Routledge.

Pasierowska, R. (2021). "I Wuz Like a Petty Dog": White Animalization of Enslaved Blacks. In: J. L. Chism, S. Craft DeFreitas, V. Robertson & D. Ryden (eds.), *Critical Race Studies across Disciplines: Resisting Racism through Scholactivism*. Lanham, MD: Lexington Books, pp. 31–50.

Pellegrin, P. (2013). Natural Slavery. In: M. Deslauriers & P. Destrée (eds.), *The Cambridge Companion to Aristotle's Politics*. Cambridge: Cambridge University Press, pp. 92–116.

Perdue, L. (2013). Hosea and the Empire. In R. Boer (ed.), *Postcolonialism and the Hebrew Bible:The Next Step*. Atlanta, GA: Society of Biblical Literature, pp. 169–192.

Perdue, L. G. (1997). The Household, Old Testament Theology, and Contemporary Hermeneutics. In: L. G. Perdue, J. Blenkinsopp, J.J. Collins, and C. Meyers (eds.), *Families in Ancient Israel*. Louisville, KY: Westminster John Knox Press, pp. 223–257.

Perry, C., D. Eltis, S.L. Engerman, and D. Richardson, eds. (2021). *The Cambridge World History of Slavery, Vol. 2: AD 500–AD 1420*. Cambridge: Cambridge University Press.

Ploeg, J. P. M. van der (1972). Slavery in the Old Testament. *Supplements to Vetus Testamentum* 22, 72–87.

Priest, J. (1852). *Bible Defense of Slavery*. Glasgow: W. S. Brown.

Rajak, T. (2000). *The Jewish Dialogue with Greece and Rome: Studies in Cultural and Social Interaction*. Leiden: Brill.

Ramelli, I. L. E. (2016). *Social Justice and the Legitimacy of Slavery: The Role of Philosophical Asceticism from Ancient Judaism to Late Antiquity*. Oxford: Oxford University Press.

Risinger, J. (2021). *Stoic Romanticism and the Ethics of Emotion*. Princeton, NJ: Princeton University Press.

Rosenfeld, B.-Z. & Perlmutter, H. (2020). *Social Stratification of the Jewish Population of Roman Palestine in the Period of the Mishnah, 70–250 CE*. Leiden, MA: Brill.

Roth-Gerson, L. (1987). *The Greek Inscriptions from the Synagogues of Eretz Israel* (Hebrew). Jerusalem: Yad Izhak Ben-Zvi.

Sandnes, K. O. (1997). Equality within Patriarchal Structures: Some New Testament Perspectives on the Christian Fellowship as a Brother- or Sisterhood or a Family. In: H. Moxnes (ed.), *Constructing Early Christian Families: Family as Social Reality and Metaphor*. London: Routledge, pp. 150–165.

Schwabe, M. & Lifshitz, B. (1974). *Beth She'arim, Vol. 2: The Greek Inscriptions*. Jerusalem: Massada Press.

Schwartz, S. (2001). *Imperialism and Jewish Society: 200 B.C.E. to 640 C.E.* Princeton, NJ: Princeton University Press.

Sheikh, F. (2019). Being an Intelligent Slave of God: Discursive Strategies and Subject Formation in Early Muslim Thought. *Journal of Religious Ethics* 47, 125–152.

Sivertsev, A. (2005). *Households, Sects, and the Origins of Rabbinic Judaism*. Leiden: Brill.

Smith, G. (1863). *Does the Bible Sanction American Slavery?* Cambridge: Sever and Francis.

Sokolov, J. A. (2010). The Antebellum Jewish Abolitionists. In: J. D. Sarna & A. Mendelsohn (eds.), *Jews and the Civil War: A Reader*. New York: New York University Press, pp. 125–144.

Sommer, B. D. (2009). *The Bodies of God and the World of Ancient Israel*. Cambridge: Cambridge University Press.

Stern, D. (1994). *Parables in Midrash: Narratives and Exegesis in Rabbinic Literature*. 2nd ed. Cambridge, MA: Harvard University Press.

Stoutjesdijk, M. J. (2020). From Debtor to Slave: An Explorative Bildfeld Analysis of Debt and Slavery in Early Rabbinic and New Testament Parables. In: M. Poorthuis & E. Ottenheijm (eds.), *Parables in Changing Contexts: Essays on the Study of Parables in Christianity, Judaism, Islam, and Buddhism*. Leiden: Brill, pp. 280–300.

Teugels, L. (2019). *The Meshalim in the Mekhiltot: An Annotated Edition and Translation of the Parables in Mekhilta de Rabbi Yishmael and Mekhilta de Rabbi Shimon bar Yochai.* Tübingen: Mohr Siebeck.

Thoma, C. (1989). Literary and Theological Aspects of the Rabbinic Parables. In: C. Thoma & M. Wyschogrod (eds.), *Parable and Story in Judaism and Christianity.* New York: Paulist Press, pp. 26–41.

Tise, L. E. (1987). *Proslavery: A History of the Defense of Slavery in America, 1701–1840.* Athens, GA: University of Georgia Press.

Urbach, E. E. (1964). The Laws Regarding Slavery as a Source for the Social History of the Period of the Second Temple, the Mishnah and Talmud, *Papers of the Institute of Jewish Studies, University College London* 1, 1–94.

Vile, J. R. (2020). *The Bible in American Law and Politics: A Reference Guide.* Lanham, MD: Rowman & Littlefield.

Visotzky, B. L. (1990). Anti-Christian Polemic in Leviticus Rabbah. *Proceedings of the American Academy for Jewish Research* 56, 83–100.

Waller, G. (2015). *A Cultural Study of Mary and the Annunciation: From Luke to the Enlightenment.* Abingdon: Routledge.

Westermann, W. L. (1955). *The Slave Systems of Greek and Roman Antiquity.* Philadelphia, PA: The American Philosophical Society.

Whitford, D. M. (2016). *The Curse of Ham in the Early Modern Era: The Bible and the Justifications for Slavery.* London: Routledge.

Wiedemann, T. E. J. (1981). *Greek and Roman Slavery.* London: Routledge.

Wilson, B. E. (2015). *Unmanly Men: Refigurations of Masculinity in Luke-Acts.* Oxford: Oxford University Press.

Yonge, C. D. (1854–1890). *The Works of Philo Judaeus, the Contemporary of Josephus, Translated from the Greek.* London: H. G. Bohn. www.earlyjewishwritings.com/philo.html.

Yuval, I. J. (2008). *Two Nations in Your Womb: Perceptions of Jews and Christians in Late Antiquity and the Middle Ages.* Berkeley, CA: University of California Press.

Zangenberg, J. K. (2016). Performing the Sacred in a Community Building: Observations from 2010–2015 Kinneret Regional Project Excavations in the Byzantine Synagogue of Horvat Kur (Galilee). In: J. Day, R. Hakola, and M. Kahlos (eds.), *Spaces in Late Antiquity: Cultural, Theological and Archaeological Perspectives.* London: Routledge, pp. 166–189.

Zeitlin, S. (1962–3). Slavery during the Second Commonwealth and the Tannaitic Period. *The Jewish Quarterly Review* 53, 185–218.

Ziegler, I. (1903). *Die Königsgleichnisse des Midrasch beleuchtet durch die römische Kaiserzeit.* Breslau: Schlesische Verlagsanstalt von S. Schottländer.

Cambridge Elements ☰

Religion and Monotheism

Paul K. Moser

Loyola University Chicago

Paul K. Moser is Professor of Philosophy at Loyola University Chicago. He is the author of *Paul's Gospel of Divine Self-Sacrifice; The Divine Goodness of Jesus; Divine Guidance; Understanding Religious Experience; The God Relationship; The Elusive God* (winner of national book award from the Jesuit Honor Society); *The Evidence for God; The Severity of God; Knowledge and Evidence* (all Cambridge University Press); and *Philosophy after Objectivity* (Oxford University Press); co-author of *Theory of Knowledge* (Oxford University Press); editor of *Jesus and Philosophy* (Cambridge University Press) and *The Oxford Handbook of Epistemology* (Oxford University Press); co-editor of *The Wisdom of the Christian Faith* (Cambridge University Press). He is the co-editor with Chad Meister of the book series *Cambridge Studies in Religion, Philosophy, and Society.*

Chad Meister

Affiliate Scholar, Ansari Institute for Global Engagement with Religion, University of Notre Dame

Chad Meister is Affiliate Scholar at the Ansari Institute for Global Engagement with Religion at the University of Notre Dame. His authored and co-authored books include *Evil: A Guide for the Perplexed* (Bloomsbury Academic, 2nd edition); *Introducing Philosophy of Religion* (Routledge); *Introducing Christian Thought* (Routledge, 2nd edition); and *Contemporary Philosophical Theology* (Routledge). He has edited or co-edited the following: *The Oxford Handbook of Religious Diversity* (Oxford University Press); *Debating Christian Theism* (Oxford University Press); with Paul Moser, *The Cambridge Companion to the Problem of Evil* (Cambridge University Press); and with Charles Taliaferro, *The History of Evil* (Routledge, in six volumes). He is the co-editor with Paul Moser of the book series *Cambridge Studies in Religion, Philosophy, and Society.*

About the Series

This Cambridge Element series publishes original concise volumes on monotheism and its significance. Monotheism has occupied inquirers since the time of the Biblical patriarch, and it continues to attract interdisciplinary academic work today. Engaging, current, and concise, the Elements benefit teachers, researched, and advanced students in religious studies, Biblical studies, theology, philosophy of religion, and related fields.

Cambridge Elements ⹀

Religion and Monotheism

Printed in the United States
by Baker & Taylor Publisher Services